OUR HEARTS REJOICE

EDITED BY

JOHN E. MEYER

THE WARTBURG PRESS, COLUMBUS, OHIO

OUR HEARTS REJOICE

Copyright 1955, The Wartburg Press

DEDICATION

To My Wife
Dorothy Fox

And to My Children
Dwight and Dorothy, Jr.

PREFACE

Holy Communion is the central act of Lutheran Christian worship.

In planning this book on this central sacrament I felt a need, a need for a book containing Lutheran teaching regarding the Sacrament of Holy Communion in clear, simple language which would serve as a constant source of information and inspiration for laymen and laywomen of the Lutheran Church.

Probably the most important thing that needs to be said about this book is that it has been published to be read frequently. That may sound trite, and yet, so many books are published, only to be read once and then forgotten. *Our Hearts Rejoice* has been prepared as a devotional manual in the hope that this will not happen. The meditations come from the pens of many men, and no one meditation will, therefore, indicate the style and the emphasis of the entire book. Truly, variety is the spice of this book, and I hope the variety is complete enough so that the reader may turn to the book hundreds of times without feeling that he has received everything it has to offer.

The twenty-four meditations found in this book are longer than are the usual meditations found in various devotional books and booklets. They are longer for a good reason. If Holy Communion is anything it is profound, and it is extremely difficult to write anything really complete about the Sacrament in a few hundred words. The authors were instructed and encouraged to write extensively enough so that, when they had finished, they would have written something which was thoroughgoing and quite inclusive.

The question remains whether Lutheran lay people will spend a little more time reading in order to get a great deal more value from the time spent. If they will, I believe this book will be of inestimable value as a source of information and inspiration as they turn their thoughts to the Sacrament of Holy Communion.

JOHN E. MEYER

April 30, 1954

CONTENTS

✦

I. A SEARCHING PREPARATION

II. A JOYFUL RECEPTION

III. A DEDICATED DEPARTURE

I

A SEARCHING PREPARATION

FOR SINNERS ONLY

By Amos John Traver

⸓ ⸓ ⸓

Read Psalm 51 and I Corinthians 11:17-34

"Let a man prove himself, and so let him eat of that bread and drink of that cup. For he that eateth and drinketh unworthily eateth and drinketh damnation to himself, not discerning the Lord's body," I Corinthians 11:28, 29.

⸓

These are strong words, shocking to any easygoing attitude toward the Sacrament of the Altar. St. Paul was terribly disturbed by reports of feasting by the Corinthians at the Communion Table. They had made the Sacrament a time of good-fellowship. There had been no sense of the real presence of the Host. They had forgotten the wounds He bore for them. They had not prepared for the gift of forgiving love by sincerely repentant hearts. If they had discerned His presence they would have come in deepest humility, crying, "God, be merciful to me, a sinner." They had failed to prove themselves, to examine themselves in the light of the cross of Christ.

Failure at any time to come before God confessing sin and deeply repentant is to shut the door of mercy. Christ came to save sinners only, to save only those who acknowledge their desperate need of a Savior. How clear is this demand in the sacrament of forgiveness! There Christ comes to us, the crucified and risen Savior. In His presence the true nature of our sin is revealed. We realize that we cannot solve the problem of our sin through any human powers. We find hope, certainty of forgiveness only in what Christ has done for us. By receiving the body and the blood of Christ in faith, we know the joy of forgiveness and find His strength to overcome the temptations that are ahead. Peace and power are Christ's gift of grace in the Sacrament. They can be ours only when we come to the Table with sincerely repentant hearts.

The Recurring Note of Repentance

The call to repent is a constantly recurring note in the gospel. It began with John the Baptist, heralding Jesus with the searching cry, "Repent, for the kingdom of heaven is at hand," Matthew 3:2. Jesus took up the refrain after the imprisonment of John and "began to preach, saying, Repent for the kingdom of heaven is at hand," Matthew 4:17; Mark 1:15. Jesus pronounced judgment on the cities of Galilee "because they did not repent," Matthew 11:20, 21. Jesus rebuked the proud Pharisees, warning them that men of ancient Nineveh will "rise up in the judgment with this generation and condemn it; for they repented at the preaching of Jonah, and behold, something greater than Jonah is here," Matthew 12:41.

The call to repentance continues in the preaching of the apostles. In his Pentecost sermon Peter said, "Repent, and be baptized, every one of you in the name of Jesus Christ for the forgiveness of your sins," Acts 2:38. At the Gate Beautiful where he and John had healed a lame man in the name of Jesus, Peter called on the astounded crowd to "repent, turn again, that your sins may be blotted out," Acts 3:19. Paul told the Athenians, "The times of ignorance God overlooked, but now He commands all men everywhere to repent," Acts 17:30. To Agrippa he declared his message to the Gentiles, "that they should repent and turn to God and perform deeds worthy of repentance," Acts 26:20. Repentance has been in the heart of the gospel from the very beginning.

When Rome adopted Christianity, it was not all victory for Christ. Multitudes accepted Christianity without experiencing real conversion. It was good policy to adopt the state religion. The Roman Church lost the historic note of repentance and substituted penance. Confession became formal. It was followed by acts of penance, prescribed by the priest, which were intended not only to show sorrow for sin but also partially to pay the debt of sin. Luther saw how this belittled God's grace and denied the fulness of Christ's sacrifice for our sin. The first of the Ninety-five Theses sounded again the emphasis of the first-century church on the need of repentance. Luther wrote, "Our Lord and Master, Jesus Christ, in saying, 'Repent ye,' intended that the whole life be penitence." God's forgiveness requires no supplementary acts on the part of the sinner. We need to come only in faith to receive God's gift of forgiveness.

Repentance, more than Sorrow

In the spring of 1518 Luther wrote his spiritual father, Staupitz, to protest the meaning given repentance by the Roman Church. It was not enough to be sorry for sins. Nor was it enough to follow sorrow with prescribed acts of penance. Luther insisted that repentance included "assuming another mind and disposition." He quoted Paul, "Be transformed by the renewal of your minds," Romans 12:2. Repentance certainly requires sincere sorrow for sin, but it goes on to a complete about-face from sin to Christ. God begins the process of repentance in our heart by His grace.

Christianity is not our search for God and our finding Him in Christ. It is God's search for us, lost in our sins. Grace is a great word, the most important word in our gospel. It means gift or favor (Ephesians 2:8). Christ comes to us in the Sacrament, offering forgiveness. Forgiveness can mean nothing to anyone who confesses no need. Repentance requires us to "prove" ourselves, to examine ourselves. The light in which we look at ourselves and our sin shines from the cross of our Lord. Only when we see the price paid for our sin do we realize the true nature of our sins. Only when we set our life against the background of Christ's perfection do we understand how we have failed God. When we realize the presence of Christ we are driven to our knees to cry, "God, be merciful to me, a sinner." In the light of all that the Sacrament means we will "examine ourselves and find nothing in us but sin and death, from which we can in no wise set ourselves free."

The root of the word "repent" is the same as that of the word "pain." It does require heartfelt sorrow. This sorrow is not self-centered. It is certainly not due to fear of punishment. Godly repentance centers in Christ. By our sins we have denied and betrayed our Savior. If we love Him, our greatest sorrow will be the thought of our betrayal of His love. We have brought suffering and death to One who loved us and gave Himself for us. We have shared in wounding Him. When we understand that Christ faces us anew in the Sacrament we must be full of contrition. The greater our love for Him, the greater our distress.

Away from Sin toward God

Christian repentance, then, turns away from sin after a clear look at its awfulness and turns toward God with His gift of forgiveness. We trust God who has promised to forgive when we come to Him humbly repentant. As we turn to God in the Sacrament we discover that His forgiveness is more than a "wiping of the slate clean" of our sins. God's grace not only cleanses our heart but makes us "fit to be called children of God." It works in us "repentance *unto life*" (Acts 11:18).

Judas, betrayer of our Lord, was desperately sorry for his sin. He did not trust the forgiving love of Christ. So suicide was the logical outcome of his sorrow. Peter failed his Lord as truly as did Judas, but he never lost his love for and his faith in Christ. The logical outcome of Peter's faith was a life ever more consistently devoted to Christ. Paul never forgot that he had persecuted the disciples of Christ, but the greater his sense of sin, the more Christ's forgiveness meant to him. He grew in grace and the knowledge of God. Judas was centered in himself. Peter, Paul, and all the great saints of Christian history were centered in Christ. They believed and found by experience that "if we confess our sins, God is faithful and just to forgive us our sins." Repentance is away from sin and toward God.

For Sinners only

The Sacrament of the Altar is "for the remission of sins." The Sacrament is one of the means through which Christ's forgiveness comes to those who love and trust Christ. All that Christ has done for us in His life and death and resurrection comes to us anew in the Sacrament. Christ "for our deliverance, suffered death and all that we by our sins have deserved." Unless we know we are sinners, this Sacrament can have no meaning for us.

Repentance is an essential of the Christian life. Confession of need must lead us to our Savior. It has been suggested that "For Sinners Only" be inscribed over every church door. The most saintly Christians have felt this. Paul called himself "chief of sinners." In the churchyard near my childhood home was the grave of one of the most saintly pastors ever to serve in the home church. By his selection on the tombstone was inscribed, "A sinner, saved by grace."

If confession of sin is essential for the entire Christian life, it is not less essential in preparation for the sacrament of forgiveness. No forgiveness is offered the sinner without repentance. Services of public confession are properly provided for those who commune. In many churches private confession to the pastor is also provided. Most important is that each communicant confess his sins directly to his God in the quiet of his own personal devotions. Only as sincerely repentant sinners dare we come to the mercy seat.

To unrepentant sinners the Sacrament is a mockery, a form without meaning. It brings condemnation, not forgiveness (I Corinthians 11:27-29). This was the double sin of those who desecrated the Lord's Table in the Corinthian church. But to all who come in faith and in love, however terribly they have sinned, the Sacrament is a means of God's grace, a channel through which God cleanses their heart of sin and strengthens them for more Christlike living. In the words of the Order for Public Confession, "Therefore whoso eateth of this bread and drinketh of this cup, firmly believing the words of Christ, dwelleth in Christ and Christ in Him and hath eternal life." So "let a man prove himself" and then throw himself unreservedly on the mercy and the love of God. The Sacrament is "For Sinners Only."

O God, our Heavenly Father, I confess unto Thee that I have grievously sinned against Thee in many ways; not only by outward transgressions, but also by secret thoughts and desires, which I cannot fully understand, but which are all known to Thee. I do earnestly repent and am heartily sorry for these my offences, and I beseech Thee of Thy great goodness to have mercy upon me, and for the sake of Thy dear son, Jesus Christ, our Lord, to forgive my sins, and graciously to help my infirmities. Amen.

—*The Common Service Book of the Lutheran Church.*

A CRY FOR MERCY

By O. A. Geiseman

⚜ ⚜ ⚜

Read Psalm 51

"Lord, I believe; help Thou mine unbelief," Mark 9:24.

⚜

The words of our text came as a cry for mercy from the lips of a troubled father. This father had a son who had been demon-possessed since early childhood. The father, distressed by his child's suffering, brought his boy to our Lord's disciples with the hope that they might free him from the bonds of the evil spirit within him. While the disciples were trying unsuccessfully to give help to the child, Jesus approached. The father then turned to our Lord and begged Him to perform the miracle in which the disciples had failed.

Jesus heard the father's plea. With His well-known understanding, sympathy, and love He assured the father that his child would be helped if he would but believe. It was then the father cried out, "Lord, I believe; help Thou mine unbelief."

Belief

This father had obviously heard of Christ's teachings and of the miracles which He had performed and by which He had brought relief to many other sufferers. He had accepted in good faith what he had learned about Jesus and

17

on the basis of this believed in Him and trusted in Him as the one who could help in his great need. He could honestly say, "Lord, I believe."

What was true of this man, by the mercies of God, is also true of you and of me. We have had the privilege of learning the wonderful story of Jesus and His love. We are quite familiar with the facts of His life. We know how He came into this world as a man by birth of the virgin Mary, and how He as the Lamb of God took all our sins upon Himself, walked the way of sorrows, and paid the price of the atoning sacrifice on the altar of the cross. We know that He did all of this for us, and we should certainly count it an insult if anyone were to suggest that we did not believe in Him. Each one of us, by the mercies of God and the work of His Holy Spirit, can truthfully say, "Lord, I believe."

Unbelief

Despite the fact that this troubled father could honestly say, "Lord, I believe," he added the cry of distress, "Help Thou mine unbelief." This, at first blush, sounds like nonsense. This seems flatly to contradict his first statement, "Lord, I believe," and yet we should miss the point completely if we gave it no further thought.

The truth is that this man's cry for help reveals the fact that the Spirit of God had given him a very keen and clear insight into his own heart. While he, under the influence of God's Holy Spirit, placed his trust in Christ, unbelief within his own natural heart was plaguing him with uncertainty and doubt so that a continuous struggle between belief and unbelief was going on within his soul.

If you and I look into our own heart and observe, as the Spirit of God provides light and understanding, we shall discover that we have just as much reason as did this dis-

tressed father to cry, "Lord, help Thou mine unbelief."
This unbelief within us manifests itself in many ways.

Have you ever stopped to think why it is that you and
I so often find ourselves gripped by fear? If you have, and
if you have thought about it in the light of God's Holy
Word and from the Christian point of view, you will have
realized that all our fears are due to the fickleness of our
faith and to our doubts. If you and I always firmly and
confidently believe that we are God's children, that God
loves us, that Jesus has redeemed us from all the powers
of evil, that God hears our prayers, and that He will not
fail us on a single promise which He has given us, then our
heart will be completely free from fear. That is what the
Bible says: "Perfect love casteth out fear." The fears we
have are evidence of the fact that we are in the same predicament in which the father found himself who cried,
"Lord, I believe; help Thou mine unbelief."

This same doubt and unbelief show themselves also in
our failure with joy and readiness to accept God's moral
guidance. Our heavenly Father has laid down certain guidelines by which we are to order our life. He did this in the
Ten Commandments which we find elaborated and explained in part by Jesus Himself in His great Sermon on the
Mount. Although as Christians we should know that God
provides these guidelines so that we might know with assurance what to do and what not to do, to the end that ours
might be a happy and a richly blessed life, we again and
again act as though this were not true. Instead of cheerfully
accepting God's way in faith we proceed as though we
knew better than God what would make for our happiness.
The result is that in our moments of doubt and uncertainty
we veer away from the pathway of God and in the spirit
of self-willed individuals pursue our own way.

In His very First Commandment God tells us that we should give first place in our heart to Him. In the Second and the Third Commandments He then makes clear to us how this is to be done. This, God would have us understand, is absolutely fundamental to a happy and satisfying life. If we put anything else into first place in our heart and assign to God a subordinated place we are bound to get things twisted in our life. Everything will become disordered and disorganized, and we are certain to find ourselves very unhappy people.

God has been good to us. We profess to believe in Him. In all honesty we say, "Lord, I believe." And yet in the realities of daily living our unbelief arises to plague us. We put other things in the place of God. We give such things as money or pleasure or fame the place of priority in our heart. God is dislodged, and something else is put into the place which rightfully belongs to Him. We do this because we believe that our sense of values is somehow better than God's, and that His judgment and His direction are not to be completely trusted, and thus we involve ourselves in the idolatrous worship of false gods.

Something similar happens with reference to all of the other commandments which God has given us, and by which He would guide us in our relationship to all other members of human society. God has said, "Thou shalt not kill." This does not mean merely that we should refrain only from actually taking someone's life, but it also means that we should have no hatred in our heart, no feelings of bitterness against our fellow men. We should rather "love our enemies, bless them that curse us, and pray for them that despitefully use us and persecute us."

Again God told us this because He loves us, and because He wants ours to be a beautiful and a happy life. Despite the fact that we say, "Lord, I believe," it is so often true that in reality we don't believe that God has told us the truth. We think that we are going to get more satisfaction out of life, that we are going to be stronger men and women, if we hate our enemies, and if we avenge ourselves as fully as possible for any wrongs which they may have done unto us. Even though man's refusal to accept God's direction in this very matter has resulted in violent conflict, in much shedding of blood, and in unutterable tragedy for countless millions of people, we still find it so very difficult to accept our Lord's direction. We believe, and yet we must at the same time cry out, "Lord, help Thou our unbelief."

We discover something quite comparable when we look to all of those directions which God has given us concerning the relationship of the sexes toward one another. God said, "Thou shalt not commit adultery." This commandment is not difficult to understand. This commandment, like the others, was given to us, not to make us miserable and to deprive us of any happiness, but quite the contrary. God gave it so that our life might be happy.

But again we have so much difficulty believing it. That is why also professed Christians will turn with avidity to movies which are deliberately designed to arouse sinful lusts; to books, pictures, and music whose underlying purpose it is to be obscene and to ignite the fires of sinful passion within the hearts of men. That explains also why professed Christians so often accept the world's point of view regarding marriage and think with such apparent indifference about the horribleness of divorce. We believe, but our heart is constantly vacillating between belief and unbelief with the result that each one of us only too often forsakes the pathway of God and goes his own way.

This matter of unbelief reveals itself also in the great crises of our life. Each one of us is likely to have those moments in life when he finds himself face to face with matters of great and grave importance. It may be that we are ordered to the hospital by our doctor to submit to surgery. It may be that we must reach a significant decision as to the choice of our vocation. It may be that we are compelled to express a judgment affecting the entire future course of our life. As Christians we know what we ought to do. We ought to pray. We ought to exercise the best judgment which God has given us, and beyond that we ought confidently to commit everything into His care with the absolute assurance that He will not fail us, and that all things must work together for good to those who love Him. Despite the fact that each one of us says, "Lord, I believe," we so often have the humiliating experience of being just as worried and as unsure in the face of these critical situations as is the rankest kind of an unbeliever. We fail God in those moments, and we fail ourselves. We simply do not apply to these specific situations in our life what we profess to believe. We act as though we did not believe.

Repentance

What has been said will suffice to help each one of us, under God, to understand how unstable we are in our spiritual life, and how far we fall short of living as believing children of God. Even as the worried father in all humility acknowledged his great need when he cried out, "Lord, help Thou mine unbelief," so have you and I every reason to stand before our heavenly Father with blushes of shame and acknowledge the many instances in which we have departed from His way and sinned against Him. The prodigal son, suffering from the consequences of his evil behavior, came back and said, "Father, I am no longer worthy to be called thy son." When you and I stand before God in the nakedness of our soul and look at all the taints and blots of sin that are upon us we can do no other.

We, too, like the publican in the Temple, must plead, "God, have mercy upon me, a sinner." Not one of us can with right boast about his goodness or lay any claim to an unswerving loyalty to God. In the light of our own performance it is plain that we are all as an unclean thing, and that all our righteousnesses are as filthy rags.

God's Gift of Love

When the troubled father cried, "Lord, help Thou mine unbelief," Jesus did not turn him aside. He heeded his words; He answered his prayer on behalf of his son and freed the poor child from the demon's power.

God's love for you and for me is no less. Jesus wanted us to be definitely sure of this fact. That is why He instituted the Holy Supper, and that is why it is such a holy and joyful privilege for me at this time to invite you to come with hungry and with pleading heart to kneel at the Lord's altar. Jesus who loves you with an infinite love, and who gave Himself into death on your behalf wants you to receive personal and direct assurance of this fact. He is eager to give to you His own body and His blood as a heavenly seal of your redemption. He wants to say to you: "Be of good cheer, my child, thy sins be forgiven thee. This is My body which was given for you. This is My blood which was shed for you for the remission of your sins." Thus Jesus, our blessed Lord, would again lift our drooping spirits and fill our heavy and sin-darkened heart with the light of His love and with that heavenly peace which surpasses all understanding.

When this peace comes, and you again marvel anew and more fully than ever before at God's inexhaustible fountain of grace and merciful goodness you will want to express your appreciation, your gratitude more clearly, more convincingly than you have done in the past. Thus Holy Communion will become to you, as a humble penitent, not only a means by which the Spirit of God restores unto you the joy of your salvation but also a means by which the same Spirit affords you new strength to live a beautiful Christian life of love and devotion.

May it please God's Holy Spirit to be with each one of you and help you to come with a humble, penitent, believing heart so that these marvelous blessings of God's love might be yours.

O God of mercy, we are sinful and desperately need Thy pardon. We truly believe that in Thy boundless love Thou wilt abundantly pardon all our trespasses. We can come before Thee only in complete unworthiness, yet, by the merits of our Christ, Thou hast accounted us worthy to behold the fulfilment of Thy precious promises, and we are grateful. By the Holy Spirit convict us of our sins and by the body and the blood of Christ cleanse us and make us pure. By Thine own power prepare us to receive this glorious Sacrament. We pray in Christ's name. Amen.

SEARCHING OUR HEART

By E. E. Ryden

⌁ ⌁ ⌁

Read II Peter 1:5-21

"Let a man examine himself, and so eat of the bread and drink of the cup. For any one who eats and drinks without discerning the body eats and drinks judgment upon himself," I Corinthians 11:28, 29.

⌁

I

The Lord's Supper is the Holy of Holies of the Christian religion. It is the only act of worship our Lord and Savior commanded His followers to observe. "Do this," said He, "in remembrance of Me." And in obedience to that command Christians have come together for nearly twenty centuries to keep this holy feast. *The* service of the Christian Church, whether it be known as the Mass, the Eucharist, the Holy Communion, or the Liturgy, is the observance of the Lord's Supper. At its very center is the Sacrament of the Altar.

When God spoke to Moses out of the burning bush at Mount Horeb He said, "Do not come near; put off your shoes from your feet, for the place on which you are standing is holy ground." And we read that Moses "hid his face, for he was afraid to look at God."

As we approach the Lord's Supper we realize that we, too, are standing on holy ground. But our Lord has invited us to this blessed feast, and we need, therefore, not come to it with fear in our heart. On the contrary, we know that He graciously welcomes every penitent soul that seeks His throne of grace, wherefore we may "draw near with a true heart in full assurance of faith." Nevertheless, we realize that, if He should enter into judgment with us according to our life and our deeds, we must confess ourselves utterly unfit and unworthy to come into His presence, much less to partake of His broken body and His precious blood. We know that He is altogether holy, righteous, just, and pure, and we acknowledge that we are altogether sinful, unrighteous, unjust, impure.

That is why, when we purpose to come to the Lord's Supper, the Word of God is so insistent that "a man examine himself, and so eat of the bread and drink of the cup. For any one who eats and drinks without discerning the body eats and drinks judgment upon himself." And that is why the church has also ordained that the celebration of the Lord's Supper shall be preceded by a preparatory service, in which the penitent soul may not only confess its sinfulness but may also receive the assurance of God's forgiveness.

This assurance, which is given by the pastor, is called absolution. It is usually spoken publicly in the preparatory service, but it may also be given by the pastor privately, e.g., at a sickbed, or when a troubled soul comes to him to make confession of a sin that rests heavily upon his conscience and robs him of peace of mind. Luther thought highly of the value of private confession and declared that he would not give it up for "all the treasures of the world." The Augsburg Confession likewise teaches that it "ought to be retained in the churches." Both Luther and the Augsburg Confession, however, agreed that, whether it be public or private, the chief spiritual value of confession *must be found in the absolution.* This comfort and this assurance, given by the church through its appointed servants to all penitent sinners, are as valid as though God Himself had spoken. This church rite is known as the Office of the Keys. It is a divine treasure possessed by the church that may never be taken from it.

On the other hand, the preparatory service is intended also to proclaim a solemn warning to the impenitent and unbelievers not to partake of the Holy Supper. This Sacrament is a *communion* of Christ with His own people. It is the true "love feast" of the Christian Church. Its purpose is to nurture the life in Christ: to work repentance in believers and to strengthen their faith. Unlike the gospel, it has not been given that it might bring the unregenerate to faith, and therefore none but such as confess Christ as Lord and Savior should be permitted to receive it.

II

Who, then, is truly worthy and well prepared to come to the Lord's Supper? Luther gives the answer in the *Catechism* when he says:

> "Fasting and bodily preparation are indeed a good external discipline; but he is truly worthy and well prepared who believes these words: 'Given and shed for you for the remission of sins.'"

These words of the great Reformer suggest to us, not only what is the great spiritual blessing offered us in the Lord's Supper, but how we are to prepare ourselves worthily to receive it.

He speaks first of an external preparation such as fasting and bodily cleansing. We know that fasting has always been associated with the thought of sorrow over sin, particularly in the Old Testament. Even for us Christians there may be some value in denying the flesh for a season in order that we may give more heed to the things of the spirit. And it is certainly right and fitting, even as the priests of the Old Covenant approached the altar of God in holy garments and only after they had washed their hands and their feet, that Christians should in like manner come to the blessed Sacrament of the Altar in modest, becoming raiment and with cleansed bodies. In the Old Testament these divinely ordained ablutions were constant reminders to the people of Israel that sin defiles the soul, and that no one can come into the presence of a holy God until it has been removed. The Christian should, therefore, ever keep in mind that, while there is certainly no thought of merit or righteousness in such external disciplines, they point very definitely to humanity's deeper and more desperate need— the cleansing of the soul.

That is why Luther insists that any genuine preparation for the Lord's Supper must center in *our acceptance* of the truth that Christ's own blood was given and shed for us for the remission of sins. *We must believe it with all our heart, and the acknowledgment of it must lead us to godly sorrow and repentance.*

Our age has sought in every way to minimize the reality of sin and the awful devastation it has wrought among men. Modern psychological terminology and thinking have changed men's attitude toward evil, and it is often regarded as merely a lesser manifestation of goodness. Instead of calling sin by its own ugly name, it is popular to talk about such things as "moral lapses," "delinquency," and "warped behavioristic patterns." But sin is the most terrible fact in human history. It is more than ignorance, more than man's inhumanity to man, more than human avarice and greed, more than social injustice. In its final essence sin is rebellion against God, flaunting His holy will, despising His authority, spurning His love, and rejecting His mercy. It was sin that wove a crown of thorns to press upon our Lord's holy brow; it was sin that shouted for His blood in Pilate's court; it was sin that at last nailed the Lord of glory to a tree.

It is needful, therefore, as we approach the Lord's Table, there to experience the wonderful love of God and His saving grace in Christ Jesus, that we realize humbly that we come as unworthy sinners. Even though we have been baptized and confirmed in His church and have confessed our faith in the Redeemer we are confronted with the sad truth that we sin daily against the commandments of God and fall far short in obedience to His will. The Scriptures tell us, "None is righteous, no, not one; no one understands, no one seeks for God. All have turned aside, together they have gone wrong; no one does good, not even one," Romans 3:10-12. If in our foolish ignorance we believe that we are somehow fairly good and respectable, and that we do not share in the deep guilt of our fellow men, such faith reveals only that we need all the more to be made conscious of our imperfection before God.

III

How shall we rightly examine ourselves that we may come to a genuine consciousness, both of our sinfulness and of our need of God's grace?

First, we should *search the Scriptures*. God has given us His blessed Word as a mirror in which we may see ourselves reflected as God sees us. The Holy Spirit would be our teacher, using the law to convict us of sin and to lead us to repentance and using the gospel to bring us to faith in Christ. We need the light of God's Word to penetrate into the darkest recesses of our life, to bring our innermost thoughts and desires into the open. We need to have our hidden motives examined before the judgment seat of God. We need to have revealed to us how much of the spirit of selfishness has become enthroned in our life, keeping us from loving God above all things and our neighbor as ourselves. Luther suggests that we ponder earnestly the Ten Commandments one by one and ask ourselves honestly how we have obeyed them. That is God's own way of searching the hearts of men. It is He who has given us this standard of moral perfection that we might learn to know ourselves as sinners.

Prayer is another aid in examining ourselves for a worthy participation in the Lord's Supper. We need to spend much time in the silence of the secret chamber alone with God, seeking the guidance of His Holy Spirit.

As we pray for the spirit of true repentance and godly sorrow because of our sins we need to ask also for deliverance from the power of sin. Here Spurgeon has a word on the true nature of repentance when he says:

> "Repentance is to leave the sins that we have done before,
>   And show that we do truly grieve by doing them no
>   more."

Thus we ought to pray for deliverance from the sin of impurity, whether of mind or body; from pride and foolish vanity; from dishonesty and falsehood; from greed and covetousness; from unkind words and unjust judgments; from selfishness and indifference to the needs of others. And as we pray for strength to overcome our sins and human frailties, so we should also beseech God that He may increase in us those virtues and Christian graces which are the work of His Holy Spirit, and which ought to be the hallmark of every true believer. The apostle Peter speaks of them as evidences of "the divine nature" in those who through faith have escaped "from the corruption that is in the world because of passion."

A greater zeal for the kingdom of God and a deeper hunger for the things of the Spirit should also be subjects of our preparatory prayers. Especially should we pray that we be not numbered among those who neglect the Blessed Sacrament and thus despise the grace of God that is offered in it. It is believed that the apostolic Christians at first observed this feast every day and later most certainly every week. What shall we say, then, of those who rarely come to the Lord's Table? Luther's stern warning is as truly justified in our age of gross carelessness and spiritual indifference as it was in his:

> "Now he who does not highly value the Sacrament shows thereby that he has no sin, no flesh, no devil, no world, no death, no danger, no hell; that is to say, he does not believe that such evils exist, although he may be deeply immersed in them and completely belong to the devil. On the other hand, he needs no grace, no life, no Paradise, no heaven, no Christ, no God, no good thing. For if he believed that he was involved in such evils, and that he was in need of such blessings, he could not refrain from receiving the Sacrament, wherein aid is afforded against such evils, and again, such blessings bestowed. It will not be necessary to compel him by the force of any law to approach the Lord's Table; he will hasten to it of his own accord, will compel himself to come, and indeed urge you to administer the Sacrament to him."

IV

A final matter of which we much speak, which is definitely connnected with our personal preparation for a worthy

reception of the Holy Sacrament, has to deal with our re-
lationships with our fellow men. Jesus says: "So if you are
offering your gift at the altar, and there remember that your
brother has something against you, leave your gift there
before the altar and go; first be reconciled to your brother,
and then come and offer your gift," Matt. 5:23, 24. And
again: "For if you forgive men their trespasses, your heavenly
Father also will forgive you; but if you do not forgive men
their trespasses, neither will your Father forgive your trespasses," Matt. 6:14, 15.

While we acknowledge that no one can "earn" or merit
God's forgiveness through any acts or deeds of his own we
also know that no one can come before God as a true penitent as long as he cherishes hatred, resentment, ill-will, or
an unforgiving spirit toward his fellow man. A forgiving
God looks for the spirit of forgiveness in those who call
themselves His children. Where such a spirit is lacking, it
is evident that we ourselves do not approach God as humble
suppliants, nor do we realize how much we ourselves need
His forgiving love. The apostle Paul gives us a beautiful
picture of a forgiving Christian when he writes to the Colos-
sians: "Put on then, as God's chosen ones, holy and beloved,
compassion, kindness, lowliness, meekness, and patience,
forbearing one another and, if one has a complaint against
another, forgiving each other; as the Lord has forgiven you,
so you also must forgive," Col. 3:12-14.

Whether we have grieved our neighbor, therefore, or
he has grieved us, we should seek reconciliation before we
come to the Confessional Service. If we have offended we
should in all meekness ask for forgiveness; if we are con-
vinced that the fault lies on his side we should, nevertheless,
make it known to him that we bear no hatred or resentment
in our heart, and that we would live at peace with him.

Jesus said, "Blessed are the peacemakers, for they shall be called sons of God." It should also be clear that no one who has wrongfully gotten property not his own should present himself at the Lord's Table until he has made every effort to make restitution to the rightful owner. Our church likewise teaches that no one who lives in habitual sin and is engaged in any business or profession contrary to law or harmful to his fellow men should receive the Holy Sacrament until he is willing to forsake his manner of life and to live and labor as becomes a Christian. Unwillingness to do this reveals an unrepentant spirit, and such a one is not a worthy communicant.

Self-examination is enjoined by the Word of God and by our church that we may look earnestly into our heart and see what manner of men or women we are. Its purpose is that we may come to a fuller realization of our human sinfulness and our absolute need of God's forgiving grace and His mercy. But it is not intended to keep truly penitent souls from the Lord's Table because of the fear of unworthiness or lack of fitness. "If in your self-examination," says a great divine, "you see sin at which you tremble, and feel how faithless has been your life and how loveless your heart, come in penitence and humility to have faith renewed at His feet and the fire rekindled at the altar." Therefore,

> "Let not conscience make you linger,
>   Nor of fitness fondly dream;
> All the fitness He requireth
>   Is to feel your need of Him."

So our plea, as we approach the Table of the Lord, is simply our helplessness and spiritual need, not our merit or our desert. And rich is the promise of our Savior: "Blessed are those who hunger and thirst for righteousness, for they shall be satisfied."

God is ever calling His people to higher, better, nobler things. He wipes out the memory of the dead past with its stained and blotted record that we may face the future with renewed hope and zeal, born of His forgiving love. He graciously permits us to forget what lies behind, and as we strain forward to what lies ahead, He urges us to "press on toward the goal for the prize of the upward call of God in Christ Jesus." It is with this goal in view that His Holy Spirit bids us pray:

"Search me, O God, and know my heart!
    Try me and know my thoughts!
  And see if there be any wicked way in me,
    And lead me in the way everlasting!" Amen.

                                        Ps. 139:23, 24.

ACCOUNTED WORTHY TO STAND BEFORE THE SON OF MAN

By George Krueger

✒ ✒ ✒

Read I Corinthians 11:26-32

"Watch ye therefore, and pray always, that ye may be accounted worthy to escape all these things that shall come to pass, and to stand before the Son of man," Luke 21:36.

✒

Once more the Lord's Day approaches and with it the privilege of kneeling before the altar of our church. In the Sacrament of the Altar we shall receive the bread and the wine. Lighted candles will remind us that it was "in the night in which He was betrayed" that the Lord Jesus Christ, who is the Light of the world, instituted what we call the Lord's Supper. As we receive the bread and the wine, His words, which have never lost their ring of authority, will be spoken by the pastor: "Take and eat, this is the body of Christ, given for thee. Take and drink, this is the blood of the New Testament, shed for Thy sins."

We are deeply conscious that Jesus Christ, the living, risen Christ, is with us according to His promise, "Lo, I am with you alway, even unto the end of the world." Of course, Jesus is true to His word, and He is truly present where two or three are gathered together in His name. Wherever His Word is preached in truth and in purity, there you will find Him, and there you will find those who have come to faith in Him.

The Jesus who is present is the real Jesus, the same Jesus who passed through all those experiences enumerated in the Second Article of the Apostles' Creed, "Conceived by the Holy Ghost, born of the Virgin Mary; suffered under Pontius Pilate, was crucified, dead and buried; He descended into hell; the third day He rose again from the dead; He ascended into heaven, and sitteth on the right hand of God the Father Almighty; from thence He shall come to judge the quick and the dead."

This is the same Jesus who was not immediately recognized by Mary in the garden, following His resurrection. It is the same Jesus whom the two men on their way to Emmaus did not recognize until He was known to them by the breaking of bread. This is the same Jesus who was able, following His resurrection, to pass into sight and out of sight at will. This is the Jesus who called Himself the Son of man, and who will judge the quick and the dead. This is the Jesus before whom we must prepare to stand.

These thoughts will indicate how exacting our preparations must be as we get ready to meet Him in His church, among His people, and at the table where we are to receive, under the bread and the wine, His body and His blood.

Our first preparations are of an outward nature. We need to make certain of the time. These are busy times, and we must arrange our work in such a way that we shall be able to lay aside our ordinary tasks and make our appearance at the service of Holy Communion. It goes without saying that we ought to be on time and to remain for the whole service.

Remember, we are to meet our Lord, and so we ought to recall the statement of Luther's *Small Catechism:* "Fast-

ing and bodily preparation are indeed a good outward dis-
cipline." True reverence for the Sacrament should find expression in cleanliness, suitable and modest dress, and
worshipful bearing.

I sometimes fear we have given so little attention to the
outward preparation that we have given offense to those
who come to the Lord's Table with us. And if we give no
attention to the outward preparation, shall we not also be
inclined to neglect the inward preparation? Is it not better
to fast than to give evidence of overeating by an offensive
breath? And other habits that we indulge in—I wonder
whether we would not make very extensive outward preparations if we really expected to meet our Lord face to face
at the Communion Table. Is not inattention to the outward
things evidence of a lack of inner readiness to meet Him
who is our life and our salvation?

Suppose we have really made ready and in these outward matters considered ourselves "worthy to stand before
the Son of man." Luther very correctly reminds us that more
is required of us than good manners and a worshipful
bearing. "But he is truly worthy and well prepared who has
faith in these words: 'Given and shed for you for the remission of sins.'"

Here is that ugly word "sin" which truly describes an
ugly condition. Sin, that barrier that stands between man
and God. Sin, that has its deep roots in an inheritance—
we call it original sin.

Full well we know that Christ has by the sacrifice of
Himself broken down the middle wall of partition. His
work is complete. Nevermore need the sacrifice of Jesus
Christ be repeated. However, let us not be blind to the fact
that we are forever picking up the rocks of that broken
barrier and rearing anew the wall that separated us from

God. We are forever bringing forth words and deeds that
are an offence to Him.

We are in a sense saved when we turn to the cross and
trust the Crucified. But it is only as we keep in the current
that streams from the cross, only as we abide in the fellowship with the Savior, only as we submit to the gracious in-
fluences of the Holy Spirit that salvation pervades our
whole being.

A part of our inward preparation should be a prayerful
review of God's law. The law does not save us, but the law
everlastingly reveals to us the will of God. A reading of
the law is prescribed in the orders of service by some
churches. In the Lutheran Church communicants are taught
to do this quietly. "Here examine yourself in the light of
the Ten Commandments, whether as father or mother, as
son or daughter, master or servant, you have been dis-
obedient, unfaithful, slothful, ill-tempered, unchaste or
quarrelsome, or whether you have injured anyone by word
or deed, stolen, neglected or wasted aught, or done any
other evil." Examine yourself thus in the light of the Ten
Commandments, and the law will become a mirror that
will reveal many imperfections. And if you can now see
your own sins dimly, think what they must look like to
Him who is called the "Lamb without blemish or spot."
You will learn to speak for yourself when you use the words
of the Psalm, "Against Thee only have I sinned, and done
this evil in Thy sight."

If the law drives us to Christ it has fulfilled its purpose.
Thus we flee to Him in our confession and humbly ask Him
to grant us absolution. How else can we hope to be "accounted worthy to stand before the Son of man"?

Are you afraid? Remember, He has invited you, "Come
unto Me, all ye that labor and are heavy laden." And has

He not promised: "Him that cometh unto Me I will in no wise cast out"? Is your heart broken? Do you think that all of your preparations are inadequate? Only He can truly prepare us for a worthy reception of this sacrament. Just come and say it with the rest of us: "Create in me a clean heart, O God: and renew a right spirit within me. Cast me not away from Thy presence: and take not Thy Holy Spirit from me. Restore unto me the joy of Thy salvation: and uphold me with Thy free Spirit."

But does this make me worthy to stand before Him? Yes, when He speaks through the mouth of His ordained servants: "And upon this humble confession which you have made, as a minister of the Church of Christ and by His authority, I declare unto you who do repent and believe in Him, the entire forgiveness of all your sins, in the name of the Father, and of the Son and of the Holy Ghost." Amen. Brother! Sister! That's it! It is freely given, take it, believe it, and come boldly to the throne of grace to find help in time of need.

However, the Lord does not simply remove something from us. He gives us something. He clothes us in His righteousness. That is really what all this talk about accepting Jesus Christ as our personal Savior means. Come and say: "Thee for my Savior let me take, My only refuge let me make, Thy wounded side." Another hymn writer caught the truth when he wrote the words:

> "Jesus, Thy blood and righteousness
> My beauty are, my glorious dress.
> Mid flaming worlds in these arrayed,
> With joy shall I lift up my head."

When the Lord makes you worthy to stand before Him, what have you to fear? To those who come prepared by His preparation He says:

"And the Spirit and the bride say, Come.
And let Him that heareth say, Come.
And let him that is athirst come.
And whosoever will, let him take the water of life
   freely," Rev. 22:17.

Thou, O Christ, hast broken down the middle wall of
partition and by Thy blood hast reconciled us to the Father.
Grant us grace that we may never fall away from Thee and
by unbelief and evil deeds rebuild the wall of sin which
will again separate us from the Father and from Thee.
Keep us in faith and in a state of grace by the help of the
Holy Ghost that we may use to our advantage Thy Holy
Word and the sacraments. Grant us grace to make all necessary outward preparation and inwardly order our life so
that we may be accounted worthy to stand before Thee,
the Son of man. Amen.

A SEARCHING PREPARATION

By C. Umhau Wolf

⚘ ⚘ ⚘

Read Micah 6:1-16

"Who is a God like Thee, pardoning iniquity and passing over transgression for the remnant of His inheritance? He does not retain His anger forever, because He delights in steadfast love," Micah 7:18.

⚘

In both the Old Testament and the New Testament the law of God sets up high requirements for the God-fearer. If one uses the Ten Commandments as a mirror he sees that he is a distorted image of the good that should be within himself. Even in the New Testament Beatitudes the standard is so high that our imperfection becomes hopeless guilt. In his pre-Reformation days Luther sought in vain to live up to the standards set by the Bible, by traditions, and by the church. On his trip to Rome he followed devoutly and earnestly every suggestion of his superiors to find relief from the burden of guilt that was his. But the more he looked at relics and kissed sacred spots, the more unworthy he felt himself to be. Even climbing the sacred stairs and kissing the step upon which Christ is reputed to have fallen did not cleanse his soul.

Luther and all men, before and after, have been tormented by the problem of guilt and reverence. Can a sinner dare to stand before God? Can one such as I come

41

to the Holy of Holies to receive the real presence of Christ? The peasant from Moresheth, Micah, asked that question about 700 years before the birth of Jesus. "With what shall I come before the Lord, and bow myself before God on high? Shall I come before Him with burnt offerings, with calves a year old? Will the Lord be pleased with thousands of rams, with ten thousands of rivers of oil? Shall I give my first-born for my transgression, the fruit of my body for the sin of my soul?" Micah 6:6, 7.

Samaria had fallen, and Jerusalem was threatened, but the prophet felt unworthy to appear before the Lord for forgiveness. His need of forgiveness and pardon was so great that his unworthiness seemed too great to be overlooked. He knew clearly that no amount of washings, fastings, sacrifices, even after the manner of Abraham and Isaac, would avail. In Psalm 51 David felt the same lack of confidence in his own acts: "For Thou hast no delight in sacrifice; were I to give a burnt offering Thou wouldst not be pleased." There are many who feel the same unworthiness in relation to the Sacrament of the Altar.

Micah asks another question a few verses later, "What does the Lord require of you but to do justice, and to love kindness and to walk humbly with your God?" Even this summation of the religious life at times condemns rather than absolves. How often are we not unjust! Too frequently we fail to show mercy, much less divine love, toward our fellow sinners. It is customary for us to cloak our sinfulness with Pharisaic pride. Is it not true that all these suggestions concerning preparation are meaningless until we have seen God? Until we've heard the "I am" we cannot understand or follow the "Thou shalt." Until we've seen the fiery bush which is not consumed we shall not take off our shoes in reverent fear. Until we've bowed beneath the cross we cannot present ourselves to God. "Nothing in my hand I bring, simply to Thy cross I cling."

The Holy Communion was not given for perfect men and women. It was not instituted for the blessing of the sinless but for the strengthening of the weak and the forgiving of the evil. The first supper was given to a motley crew of persons, some proud, some meek, others doubtful and even treacherous. The Sacrament is not a reward to the holy but a gift of grace to those who need it the most— the sinners.

The Lord's requirements for the perfect life are not met, but the Lord's remission is met in this Holy Communion. The very name of the prophet Micah signifies the depth of his conviction concerning the nature of his God. In Hebrew Micah signifies, "Who is like Jah (or Jehovah)?" So our text. "Who is a God like Thee, pardoning iniquity and passing over transgression for the remnant of His inheritance?" If Samaria fell because of its sins, surely Jerusalem should likewise fall, and we also. But Micah knew a God who would assuredly pardon. Other gods couldn't even hear prayers for pardon, they couldn't understand our dread fears. But this God who brought Israel from Egypt and raised Jesus from the grave can forgive and forget. He is long-suffering as Micah's question implies: "Is the Spirit of the Lord impatient?"

The steadfast love of God brought prophet and evangelist into the world. But it also gave Jesus and through Him the means of grace preserved in the church. Christ's words of institution link the loving act of God's gift to our ultimate forgiveness. "Given for you . . . shed for you . . . for the remission of sins." Through the cross the evil has been crushed, our guilt is eliminated. He will again have compassion upon us, He will tread our iniquities under foot. "Thou wilt cast all our sins into the depths of the seas." Who is a God like this? What other God gives so much and demands only repentance and humility?

In our preparation for Holy Communion we must put the emphasis, not on our unworthiness, but on God's gracious acts. "O My people, what have I done to you?" Besides the historical deliverances of Israel and the miracles of Jesus' day we now have the continued miracle of saving grace through the Word and the sacraments. Through the Word and the sacraments "you may know the saving acts of the Lord."

How can there be such a connection between God's words and our needs? "Do not My words do good to him who walks uprightly?" The words spoken in love at the Communion Table are the mightiest words on earth, for they lift the burdens from the hearts of sinners. Through these words and this presence the true meaning of the incarnation and the promised Immanuel is realized. In Micah's day the proud often rested on past laurels and righteousnesses for security and peace. "Is not the Lord in the midst of us?" Micah understood that God's coming to such people would mean only judgment. But today, through the Lord's Supper, we realize the same blessing which came to Mary. Unworthy and sinful, God comes and overpowers us and makes us His own. Even our coming is His grace and not our work.

As we prepare ourselves for the Sacrament of the Altar, Micah helps us to ask searching questions. We recognize with him that we are unworthy to come before the Lord, but in humble faith we acknowledge that there is no God like our God, "pardoning iniquity and passing over transgression."

Lord, our heavenly Father, we thank Thee for the words of prophets and evangelists which show us the inadequacies of our life, the evil of our heart, and the guilt of our mind. We acknowledge our rebellion and our unworthiness before Thee. We know that there is nothing we can do to secure Thy pardon, so we cast ourselves wholly upon Thy mercy. Receive us, O Lord Jesus, and dwell in our midst even as Thou didst not despise the publicans and the sinners. Forgive us our manifold transgressions, known and unknown, that we may be unafraid in Thy presence. And may it be that we shall rise from this place cleansed and renewed by Thy sacramental power and grace. Come Lord Jesus, be our guest. Amen.

THE CONSECRATION

By John O. Lang

⚹ ⚹ ⚹

Read Matt. 26:26-28; Mark 14:22-24; Luke 22:19, 20;
I Cor. 11:23-25

"The cup of blessing which we bless," I Cor. 10:16.

⚹

It was Thursday evening, the fourteenth day of the Jewish month of Nisan and the night for eating the Passover. In an upper room at Jerusalem, Jesus and His disciples were gathered around a table, and on that table was the *matzoth*, the unleavened bread of the Jews; here was the paschal lamb, roasted and ready to eat; here was the cup of grape wine, and near it the bitter herbs. The little band began the sacred celebration with a prayer and then started to eat that lamb without spot and without blemish, a type of Christ, the Lamb of God that taketh away the sin of the world. They ate of the *matzoth*, the unleavened bread, which reminded them that sin is like a leaven which will soon eat its way through the entire being of man and must, therefore, be purged out. They chewed on the bitter herbs and were thus reminded of the bitterness of the lot of their forefathers in Egypt, and the cup of grape wine was passed around, and they all drank of it and thus signified that they were one with each other and with the Lord. It was the last Passover meal that Jesus ate with His disciples.

46

When the Passover feast was over, Jesus took of that *matzoth* or unleavened bread which was left over and blessed it and gave it to His disciples and said, "This is My body." He then took the cup of grape wine, that same cup which only a few moments previous had been used in the Passover, and which still was not empty, and He blessed it and gave it to the disciples and said, "This is My blood." The Passover, the sacred feast of the Old Testament, was superseded by the New Testament Sacrament of our Lord's body and blood.

Just what words did Jesus use as He blessed the bread and the wine on that Thursday evening? We do not know; the words have not been recorded; the sacred record merely states, "He took bread and blessed it." We do know, however, that after Jesus had ascended into heaven, and His disciples continued to celebrate the Holy Communion, they, too, pronounced some kind of a blessing over the bread and the wine before they distributed it, for in I Corinthians 10:16 we find the familiar words, "The cup of blessing which *we bless*." What words the apostles used again we do not know, for they, too, are not recorded, but in I Timothy 4:5 we read that food "is sanctified by the Word of God and prayer."

In our Communion service we have what is known as the Consecration of the Elements. When we consecrate anything we set it aside for sacred use. This consecration is done according to apostolic usage "by the Word of God and prayer." The prayer which we use is the Lord's Prayer, that prayer which Jesus Himself has taught us. We do not merely recite this prayer as a sort of a charm over the elements; Jesus never intended for us to use a prayer in this fashion. The pastor speaks the words, and the congregation responds with a choral "Amen," and we mean each word as it is spoken, and we bring those seven humble petitions before the throne of grace.

Now comes the Word, the reciting of the words of institution as they are given us by Matthew, Mark, Luke, and St. Paul in First Corinthians. The words of institution as we find them in the Common Service are a sort of composite of the four accounts much like the Passion History which we read during Lent. By reciting these words we set aside the bread and the wine for a sacred use, and we connect up our celebration of the Holy Communion with that celebration in the upper room at Jerusalem some nineteen hundred years ago.

The Church of Rome has distorted this act of consecration and has made of it a sort of magic by which bread and wine are changed into the body and the blood of our Lord. Rome asserts that, when the priest pronounces the sacred words, "This is My body," and, "This is My blood," a miracle takes place, and the bread is no longer bread and the wine no longer wine, but rather the body and the blood of Christ. The priest speaks the words in the Latin language, and in Latin they read *"Hoc est corpus meum," "Hoc est sanguis meus,"* and from this miraculous Latin formula are derived the English words, "hocus pocus," words which are used to describe the attempt to work wonders by the reciting of magical formulas.

Out of Roman Catholic doctrine grows Roman Catholic practice. Since the bread and the wine have been changed into the body and the blood by the act of consecration, the people bow down before that consecrated wafer in adoration and worship; the cup is withheld from the laity for fear a drop of the sacred blood of Christ might be spilled; in case of fire some priest or monk or nun will invariably risk his or her life to rescue the sacred wafers from the "tabernacle" on the altar so that the body of Christ will not be consumed by the flames.

Lutherans do not believe in "transubstantiation" or the changing of the bread and the wine into the body and the blood of Christ by the reciting of the words of institution. In I Corinthians 11:26, 27, what we eat is still called "bread," which would not be the case according to Roman Catholic doctrine. To a Roman Catholic it may look like bread, smell like bread, feel like bread, and taste like bread, but it is not bread; it is the body of Christ. However, though Lutherans do not believe in "transubstantiation" they do believe that together with the bread and the wine we do receive the true body and the blood of Christ in the Holy Sacrament. For in each of the four accounts of the institution Jesus says, "This is My body," "This is My blood," and not, "This represents My body," and, "This represents My blood." Since Lutherans do teach that we receive the true body and blood of Christ together with the bread and the wine in the Sacrament, some have accused us of teaching something that we do not teach. It has been asserted that Lutherans teach that by the act of consecration the body of Christ becomes imbedded in or mixed with the bread, and the blood of Christ becomes mingled with the wine. This doctrine is known as "consubstantiation," and while Lutherans are often accused of teaching it, it is not the Lutheran doctrine of Holy Communion. Consubstantiation would make of the consecration again a sort of magical formula by which the body and the blood of Christ would enter the elements of bread and wine. Lutherans are not given to magical formulas, and no real Lutheran believes in consubstantiation.

Over against the Reformed churches which see in the Sacrament a mere symbolism of Christ's body and His blood we Lutherans hold to the doctrine of the "real presence," but it is not the reciting of the words of institution which put Christ's body and His blood into the Sacrament. The necessary part of every Communion Service is the "eating and drinking" without which there would be no Sacrament, and only as we *eat* of that bread do we receive Christ's body, and only as we *drink* of that wine do we receive Christ's blood. One of our German Lutheran theologians, Leonard Hutter, has aptly said: "No sacramental union takes place until the external use is added, which consists in eating and drinking; so that if the words of the institution were recited a thousand times, and this use, i.e., the eating and drinking, were not added, there still would be no sacramental union of the bread with the body or the wine with the blood of Christ." Lutherans do use the term "sacramental union" of the body and the blood with the bread and the wine, and this term merely means a union unique in the Sacrament, and it is only in the eating and the drinking that this union takes place, for without the eating and the drinking there is no Sacrament. By the act of consecration we merely set aside the elements for a holy use, and we connect up our celebration with that which Christ instituted in the upper room at Jerusalem in the same night in which He was betrayed, so that, when we *use* those elements as Christ intended us to use them, namely, by distributing them that men might eat and drink, they bring us Christ's body and His blood. As the elements lie on the altar after consecration they are merely elements set aside for a holy use, and those which remain after the distribution are merely elements left over after a holy use, but when we *receive* them, they bring us the true body and blood of our Lord.

Our Lutheran teaching concerning the Lord's Supper might be illustrated by the figure of a wire and electricity. A wire is not electricity though, if properly connected, it may bring electricity, but all the time it is bringing that electricity it is still a wire, and after it is disconnected it is only a wire. The wire may be compared with the elements of bread and wine, and the electricity with the body and the blood of Christ. The words of institution connect up the wire with the ceremony instituted by our Lord some nineteen hundred years ago so that *in the distribution* they bring us Christ's true body and His blood. When the distribution is ended, the connection is broken, and what remains is just the elements of bread and wine. We dispose of these elements reverently since they were elements used in a sacred celebration, and we, as a rule, either pour the wine back into the container or pour it out upon the ground rather than throw it into the sewer drain, but we do this only because we want to deal reverently with that which served a divine purpose and not because we believe that we are dealing with the blood of Christ.

The consecration is no magical formula by which a miracle of "transubstantiation" nor even a miracle of "consubstantiation" is effected, but it does serve an important purpose: it sets aside the elements of bread and wine for a sacred use, and it connects up our celebration with that which Christ instituted nineteen hundred years ago, and we go in spirit with Him to the upper room at Jerusalem and become His guests at that most sacred celebration this side of heaven.

Dearest Lord Jesus, as the candles are lighted to remind us of those candles which burned in the upper room in Jerusalem on that sacred night before Thy Passion, and as the holy words of institution are read by Thy minister, may our thoughts go back to that blessed moment when Thou didst take the bread and bless it and give it to Thy disciples and say, "Take eat, this is My body," and that equally blessed moment when Thou didst take the cup, give thanks, and give it to Thy disciples and say, "This is My blood of the New Testament." May no doubts arise in our mind concerning this Holy Sacrament, but may we receive it as Thine own body and blood, given and shed for us for the remission of our sins, and in this Sacrament may we be strengthened in faith toward Thee and in love toward our brethren of mankind. Hear us, O merciful Savior, for Thy love's sake, who livest and reignest with the Father and the Holy Ghost, ever one God, world without end. Amen.

PREPARATION FOR COMMUNION

By Wm. L. Young

✦ ✦ ✦

Read I Corinthians 11:23-29.

"Let a man examine himself, and so let him eat of that bread and drink of that cup," I Corinthians 11:28.

✦

I think a layman like myself should prepare for Communion reverently, thoughtfully, joyfully, frequently, expectantly, and thankfully.

We laymen should prepare reverently, for Communion is a heavenly mystery. According to God's Word we receive in the Holy Supper something earthly, namely, bread and wine, and something heavenly, namely, Christ's body and His blood—His true body which on the cross was given into death for us, and His true blood which He shed for the forgiveness of our sins. I believe this because my Lord said so.

Here is mystery beyond my comprehension and my understanding. I don't explain it because I cannot, but I accept it as fact just as I know that the soil of my garden can produce a Crimson Glory rose, and from invisible atoms scientists can manufacture atomic bombs.

I do not believe that the bread and the wine are changed to body and blood as do my Catholic neighbors. Neither do I believe that eating the bread and drinking the wine are just symbols of something or typify something as do some of my Protestant friends. I believe that in a real but heavenly manner each communicant in, with, and under the bread and the wine also receives the sacrificial body and blood of Christ, and that the necessary earthly elements which I eat and drink are sacramentally united with the heavenly elements. Since Communion is a heavenly mystery and a divine privilege, I should prepare reverently.

The words of an old hymn keep ringing in my ears:

> Full of reverence at Thy Word,
> Lord, I near Thy hallowed board;
> Mindful of Thy latest breath
> And Thy sacrificial death;
> Mediator, who for me
> Diedst from wrath to set me free,
> May I as Thy worthy guest
> By this feast of life be blest.

We laymen should prepare thoughtfully, for Communion has important meanings. My Savior says, "This is My body which is given for you—this cup is the new testament in My blood which is shed for you for the remission of sins."

Note how personal this is—"given *for you*"—"shed *for you*." When I face my real self I know I am a sinner. I know that God knows it, too. But I know that God so loved the World (and that includes me) that He gave His only-begotten Son, that whosoever (and that means me) believeth on Him should not perish but have everlasting life. My Savior died on the cross *for me*—His blood was shed *for me* for the remission of *my sins*. In my need and my selfishness I need to know that He did it *for me*, without any worthiness in me, just as He did it for all sinners like me.

> "In my hands no price I bring,
> Simply to Thy cross I cling."

There is another meaning I must not miss: My Savior says, "This do in remembrance of Me." Does He fear that we shall deny Him as did Peter, betray Him as did Judas, desert Him as did the disciples in His hour of crisis? What more intimate tug at the heart can there be than His hesitant question to His disciples, "Will ye also go away?" Time tends to heal all wounds, and often the dead are too soon forgotten. We must not forget our Lord and His death on the cross, and that He rose again from the dead. He is our living Lord. In this sacrament we must remember, as Paul tells us, that as we eat this bread and drink this cup we are proclaiming the death of the Lord *till He come.* We are remembering His whole sacrificial act for the frequent forgiving of our sins, "as oft as ye drink it."

When our Lord tells us, "This do in remembrance of Me," this command converts the first Lord's Supper as instituted by our Lord into a sacramental memorial that should be celebrated frequently. Almost as an echo of the Passover rite with its admonition, "This day shall be unto you for a memorial," comes a greater memorial, our Lord's Supper with its directive, "This do in remembrance of Me."

We laymen should prepare joyfully for Communion. Here is a privilege, an opportunity, a blessing from our Lord. In this sacrament there is forgiveness of sin, life, and salvation. For this reason joyfully I go to the Holy Supper, refreshing my hungry and thirsty soul through the enjoyment of this blessing of my Savior and receiving new strength to live in fellowship with Him and the brethren.

My joy is not in contrast with my reverence and my thoughtfulness. Physical preparation for Communion I believe should be simple—merely a clean body neatly and appropriately attired. Personally I do not favor fasting nor extended isolation before participating. I want my pastor

and my family to know that I am going to Communion today, and that it is an event of major importance. But I do
believe in thorough spiritual preparation and examination.
Paul tells us, "Let a man examine himself, and so eat of that
bread and drink of that cup." My first examination must
confirm me that I have faith in my Lord and in this sacrament. My seconl examination must confirm me that I have
removed from my heart hate of any brother, and that I
have forgiven him as I expect my Lord to forgive me. My
Christian duty is clear—if I harbor a grudge against my
neighbor I must go to him and become his friend again.
My third examination should lead me to true contrition,
sorrow, and repentance for my many sins and failures. I
must recognize these, but they must not drive me to the
despairing cry of the young Luther in his monastic cell,
repeating over and over again in the words of the Twenty-
second Psalm, "My God, why hast Thou forsaken me!" God
has not forsaken me. Christ on the cross is my cure. Happily
I go to His Holy Supper to receive forgiveness for all my
sins and failures.

> Thy table I approach,
> Dear Savior, hear my prayer:
> O let no unrepented sin
> Prove hurtful to me there.

I think we laymen should go frequently to Communion.
I am blessed in a church home where this privilege is offered frequently. My minister at Communion administers
the sacrament with fitting dignity and reverence. He does
not hurry his words or his administration, and somehow or
other I feel that here is a priest of God properly adminis-
tering this solemn sacrament. He makes me feel, though
our Communions are very large, that this Communion very

definitely was meant for me. As I take Communion, on either side of me are men and women who believe as I do and solemnly and joyfully are receiving the same blessings that I am. I am thankful that our organist plays beautifully the proper music as a background, and that our altar and our church in every way are appropriate for this sacrament.

But you may ask, "How frequently?" I think it should be more frequently than your usual custom, and I doubt whether it should be by custom only. Surely, those who commune only once a year, say on Good Friday or Easter, are not going as frequently as they should. On the other hand, we should not go so frequently and so nonchalantly that the Lord's Supper becomes cheap, common, and insignificant, but we should go frequently enough to receive richly this profound blessing, and our going should be significant and important to us. A learned friend who is a grammarian of the original tongue tells me that the direction, "This do in remembrance of Me," really means, "This do in remembrance of Me again and again."

We laymen should go to Communion expectantly and thankfully. Here we receive the cure for the greatest sickness of the world. Heathen make long pilgrimages, lash themselves, offer living sacrifices, all in vain search for the forgiveness of sins. Our Lord died on the cross for our sins, and because of our faith in Him we receive the forgiveness of sins in His Supper. Here we remember His death, strengthen our faith, and go back to our work to confess Him before men and to serve Him.

> "O may I never fail
> To thank Thee day and night
> For Thy true body and true blood,
> O God, my peace and light."

A JOYFUL RECEPTION

WHERE PAST AND FUTURE UNITE

By Wm. D. Streng

⚹ ⚹ ⚹

Read Psalm 136

"And He said unto them, 'I have earnestly desired to eat this passover with you before I suffer; for I tell you I shall never eat again until it is fulfilled in the kingdom of God,'"

Luke 22:15, 16.

⚹

It is a commonly accepted truth that children look into the future while the aged look into the past. The youth dreams of what he will be and do someday, the aged speak of what they experienced in the past.

Is there no happy combination of the two? It is a bit sad always to be living in the past, and it is so visionary only to think of the future. Neither makes for vibrant living now.

In the Sacrament of Holy Communion we have that happy fusion of past and future. It rests entirely on great events of the past—His death and His resurrection—but it also points constantly to the future, "until He come." And for me, who am a part of the present, this sacrament is the greatest gift that heaven and earth have to offer now. Every Sunday is, of course, a great day, but as some stars shine brighter than the rest, so those days when I receive His body and His blood stand out above all others. As children who have opened their Christmas gifts will usually, after the initial excitement is over, concentrate on one, the one which they treasure most, so we, able to choose among

61

many of God's wonderful gifts, choose this one as the best of them all. It brings my Savior to me here and now so that the testament which He made long ago is still new.

How, then, can this Sacrament be anything but joyful? Has not this been the center of man's endless search, to distill out of the past what is really of value and to be assured of happiness in the future?

"They saw God and did eat and drink," Exodus 24:11. That happens when we are happy. Jesus echoes this truth when He states, "Blessed [happy] are they which do hunger and thirst after righteousness, for they shall be filled."

We cannot deny it, we all live partially in the past. When we go down memory's lane we are reminded of the carefree days of childhood, the pleasant moments in the family circle, the unforgettable experience that was ours at the confirmation altar. But there are also dark pages in our past which we cannot ignore or erase.

There is a reason the happiest Christians in every congregation are those who come sincerely and frequently to the Lord's Supper. They may come as sad sinners, but after finding His forgiveness they eat and drink again.

In the future much appears dark, all of it uncertain, except for this one assurance that Christ is at my side. If His Holy Supper strengthens my fellowship with Him it is a satisfying and comforting experience, to be sure.

God Is Primary

We shall find Holy Communion a joyous experience if we center our thoughts on God and not on ourselves. I come confessing, that is true, I am reminded of the myriad of sins that have been charged against me, in the aggregate they are so numerous and so varied that it would be impossible to enumerate them.

But I can become so preoccupied with my own worthiness that I forfeit the element of praise and thanksgiving. As I approach His Sacrament I center my thoughts on Him. And that prompts me to lift up my heart. What a wonderful God we have! Micah, in his day, threw out a challenge to all the deities of neighboring nations, saying, "Who is a God like unto Thee?" What makes our God great? "That pardoneth iniquity, and passeth by transgression, retaining not His anger forever, because He delighteth in mercy," Micah 7:18. This is His crowning glory, and this is the joy of my life.

> Great God of wonders! all Thy ways
> Are worthy of Thyself—Divine
> But the bright glories of Thy grace
> Beyond Thine other wonders shine.
> Who is a pardoning God like Thee,
> Or who has grace so rich and free?
> —*Samuel Davies.*

Now while I lament the past I can also rejoice in it, for there stands my Savior still saying, "Courage, My son, your sins are forgiven," Matthew 9:2, Moffatt. After the prodigal son had returned and had been accepted again into the family circle, the fatted calf was made ready, for now it was time to rejoice.

Jesus Calls Us

Christ is concerned that I come. "And He said unto them, 'With desire I have desired to eat this passover with you before I suffer: For I say unto you, I will not any more eat thereof, until it be fulfilled in the kingdom of God,'" Luke 22:15, 16.

It is an error in perspective to think that the Sacrament of the Supper is offered because the congregation by official vote determined that this be done on certain Sundays.

It is here because our Lord desires this intimate communion with His followers. It rests upon His institution, and it is His desire that we come. Such an experience is like that of the two disciples on the way to Emmaus. Their hearts burned within them when He made Himself known to them in the breaking of bread. The preached Word is often mingled with human imperfections, but that which is received in the Sacrament is purely divine. Rather than on the incidentals, our focus ought to be on the healing, cleansing, transforming power of the Lord's Supper. Here the fundamental dilemma of worship, that I am asked to give what I cannot give, is resolved, for now I offer Him His own body and blood, which He gave for me. My inadequacy is no more, for now I plead His love, His pain, His death, and He gives me back my self-respect.

> For lo! between our sins and their reward
> We set the passion of Thy Son, our Lord.
> —*William Bright.*

Union in Communion

Unity and fellowship bring joy into our daily life. Never is our happiness quite as complete as when we are in the company of our dearest and best friends. Occasionally we drive many a mile, past hundreds of houses, to enter one particular home. There dwell those we love and cherish.

While the Sacrament of the Lord's Supper unites us with our heavenly Friend it also offers the closest possible fellowship with those who are one with us in the faith.

Sometimes at social gatherings we sense a difference in culture and in education which we find it difficult to bridge. But at this rail the incidental accidents of birth, of family, of native intelligence, of color and education are obliterated and forgotten, for here we are all one. Though we often hear it said that "all men are brothers," this statement is true only when "all are one in Christ Jesus." Only He can impart the indispensable binding element that cements mankind into a brotherhood.

The Lord's Supper is a family meal. It was closely associated with the Passover which satisfied a similar need in the religious experience of the ancient Hebrews. For the Passover Jewish families gathered to thank God for their deliverance as a nation—a joyous occasion, to be sure.

While the Eucharist unites us with the whole Christian Church, the Communion of Saints, the closest circle is that of our own household. Though we know little about the details that surrounded this Sacrament in the early church we gather that the celebration of the Lord's Supper in the days of the apostles was usually held by a large household coming together to rejoice in God and in their Christian fellowship with each other.

Unity of Life

What a therapeutic agent the Sacrament of the Lord's Supper is! Everywhere lives are falling apart so that psychiatrists, doctors, pastors are called upon for counsel.

If only we would find the unity for our life that is offered to us in this Sacrament, "for where there is forgiveness of sins, there is life and salvation." In the midst of his discussion of the Lord's Supper, especially as it concerns those who do not discern the pre-eminence of this Sacrament which offers the body of our divine Redeemer, Paul insists, "That is why many of you are weak and ill, and some have died," I Corinthians 11:30. Whatever else these words may mean they also indicate the healing power of this Sacrament. A soul that is ill has little positive influence upon the human body.

O God unseen, yet ever near,
Thy presence may we feel:
And thus, inspired with holy fear,
Before Thine altar kneel.
Thus would we all Thy words obey,
For we, O God, are Thine
And go rejoicing on our way,
Renewed with strength divine.

It has always been thus. When spiritual chaos reigned among the chosen nation of the Old Testament, we read repeatedly, "And they destroyed their altars." But when they returned to God, the writers of Holy Writ add, "And they built altars unto the Lord." There is the source of healing and of strength.

Food of Pilgrims

The early church maintained its emphasis on this Sacrament also because of her living hope in Christ's return. The Sacrament is both, a memorial of the past and a hope in the future. Already in Paul's day the Communion liturgy in all probability included the prayer, "Come, Lord Jesus!" For that reason this supper has been called a "food for pilgrims," pilgrims on the way but not yet at the goal.

The church has witnessed and projected much social progress since the days of Paul. Especially in our day have we become keenly aware of the fact that our creeds, if they are living documents, must issue in deeds. And when we realize how much remains to be done we pray with increased fervency, "Thy kingdom come." In the Lord's Supper also we are reminded of our social responsibility since the lofty sentences of our Comunion liturgy are in the plural.

However, freedom from fear and want, freedom from sin and suffering, are not to be attained fully on this side of the stars. Hence especially to the faithful the promise of our Lord's return and of eternal life is among the sweetest comforts offered in the gospel. This central doctrine of our Lord's coming again we cannot forget as we receive His body and His blood, "for as often as ye eat this bread and drink this cup, ye do show the Lord's death till He come." His own find life's deepest joy in the promise of eternal life. "This do in remembrance of Me," explains Martin Luther, "means nothing more than to preach, give thanks and be happy," (Luther's Works, St. Louis Edition, VI, 1818).

While each celebration of the Holy Supper offers us God's greatest gift out of the past it is also an anticipation of what He has in store for us in the future. The Lord's followers will continue to eat this bread and drink this cup "till He cometh." Then our joys will be complete.

Almighty and everlasting God, we most heartily thank Thee that Thou hast given to us these holy mysteries, Thy most precious body and blood. We bless Thee for the assurance given to us in the Holy Supper of Thy favor and goodness toward us. We praise Thee that Thou hast accepted us as members of the mystical body of Thy Son, the blessed company of all faithful people.

Assist us, we pray, with Thy grace that we may continue in that holy fellowship and do such good works as Thou dost require of us.

Restore again to us the joy of Thy salvation. With gladness and singleness of heart lead us to Thy altar where Thou dost give Thyself to us. Grant us for our daily tasks that serenity and peace which come from living close to Thee so that, bearing about with us the infection of a cheerful heart, we may diffuse Thy grace. Finally grant us to meet all ills and death itself with a courage and a hope that only Thou dost give; through Christ Jesus, our Lord. So be it. Amen.

WHERE DO WE GO?

By W. A. Poovey

ℐ ℐ ℐ

Read John 1:1-18.

"And the Word became flesh and dwelt among us, full of grace and truth; we have beheld His glory, glory as of the only Son from the Father," John 1:14.

ℐ

There is an old story about a young man who took a ride on the merry-go-round. Gaily he whirled on the back of a prancing animal while the music pounded out its rhythmic beat until at last all the young man's funds were exhausted. Then as he left the carnival grounds, a friend demanded to know: "You've spent your money, and where've you been?"

Of course, the story points up the meaninglessness of much human endeavor. We go through a lot of motions. There are noise and hubbub. But when it is all said and done, where have we been? Unless we are careful, human existence begins to resemble a ride on a merry-go-round or takes on the pattern described by Macbeth: "Full of sound and fury, signifying nothing."

Even in the spiritual realm such a danger is ever present. Religious people are often tempted to go through the motions of a ceremony and to repeat again and again the same pattern of worship without asking the purpose behind it all. If you ask, "Where have you been?" they cannot tell you, for they have been treading in the path of useless custom.

Has Holy Communion become a meaningless ceremony like that? God forbid! Yet one wonders if all the partakers know what it means when they come to the altar at a Communion service. Of course, worshipers in the Lutheran Church have been told repeatedly that they receive the body and the blood of Christ in the Sacrament, yet how deep are the understanding and appreciation of that which is embodied in this great worship service? Where *do* we go when we walk from our place in the church to the altar to receive the sacred elements? If we know the answer to that we shall be blessed in our worship.

Well, first of all, *we kneel beside a manger* that cradles the Son of God. Does it seem strange to imply that there is a close connection between Christmas and Holy Communion? It shouldn't. For it was at Bethlehem that "the Word became flesh and dwelt among us." It was in a manger that the Son of the living God was first manifest as Jesus, a man of body and blood.

Body and blood. Those two terms should provide the link for us between the nativity and the Sacrament of the Altar. Somehow we have tended to spiritualize part of the elements of Communion until we have lost sight of their true significance. Bread and wine are earthly, we say, forgetting that body and blood are also of this earth even when joined to the divine nature of Christ. It is precisely because the Word became flesh and dwelt among us that Jesus can give us these divine elements in Holy Communion. We dare never forget that our Savior is not a disembodied spirit hovering over us but the Son of man as He proclaimed Himself to be. And each time we come to the Sacrament we announce that truth to ourselves and to all who are willing to listen. In his book *The Presence,* the Rev. B. von

Schenk says: "Communion is the bulwark of our faith in Bethlehem and in the Incarnation of our Lord. Every time we receive the communion we confess to the faith that this little Babe is Mary's Son and God's Son."[*]

Every child loves to sing Luther's Cradle Hymn, "Away in a manger." When we grow older we are inclined to turn to more sophisticated or adult hymns. Yet when the call comes to approach the altar and receive the Sacrament, it should take us back to the song and the faith of our childhood, for we are invited to kneel by a manger and receive the body and the blood of our Lord who was manifested in the flesh in the little town of Bethlehem.

Each time we come to Communion *we are also invited to sit at a table in an upper room in Jerusalem.* Some churches have tried to re-create the scene of the first celebration by gathering the congregation around tables and by reintroducing the ceremony of footwashing. But our mind can transport us to Jerusalem very quickly without any use of physical props. So when we come to the Lord's Supper, the walls of the church should melt away, and we should feel transported to an upper room where the Master instituted this Sacrament.

For Holy Comunion has no meaning apart from that room. The fact that the Christian Church has repeated this ceremony for almost two thousand years means nothing apart from that room. Our faith that Christ is truly present in the Sacrament rests upon the words that He spoke in that room, for He said: "Take, eat, this is My body; take, drink, this is the new testament in My blood." We continue to practice this strange form of worship only because Jesus said, "This do in remembrance of Me."

---

[*] B. von Schenk, *The Presence.* Quoted by permission of the publisher, Ernst Kaufmann, Inc.

How bitterly the Christian Church has wrangled over the centuries concerning the interpretation and the meaning of Holy Communion! The history of our religion might have been so different if men had only remembered the upper room and the simple, beautiful words of the Master. For the meaning of Communion is not a matter of argument, of high-powered theological discussion and dialectic. It is a matter of faith and trust in the words of Him who has never deceived us in any of His promises. That is why, when we come to the Lord's Table, we must be transported to the upper room in Jerusalem, for there the doubts and the sophistry of the world are swept away by the gentle hands of Him who said, "Take, eat; take, drink!"

> Thy body and Thy blood,
> Once slain and shed for me,
> Are taken at Thy table here.
> O wondrous mystery!

On the altar of almost every Lutheran church there is to be found a cross. If it serves no other purpose, the symbol should remind us as we come to the Lord's Table that *we also stand beneath the cross of Calvary*. For the Lord said, "This do in remembrance of Me" when He instituted the Sacrament. When our thoughts turn to His sacrifice of body and blood, the vision of Calvary swirls before our eyes.

See the brow, crowned with thorns. See the blood flow from the five wounds of His body. Remember that it was for our sins that His precious life was offered up, and that it was through this sacrifice that we receive "power to become the children of God."

"This do in remembrance of Me." How can we ever forget? How can we stop thinking for a moment about the greatness of His sacrifice? It should be in our mind and our prayers every day, for our whole relationship to God depends on what happened at Calvary.

Yes, in this sacrament Jesus portrayed for all time a picture of His suffering and His atoning death so that men might never forget. Like a motion picture camera that has been stopped to freeze a single scene on the screen, Holy Communion focuses our attention on the suffering Savior. Here is His body, broken for us; His blood, shed for us. We dare never forget!

> Upon that cross of Jesus
> Mine eyes at times can see
> The very dying form of One
> Who suffered there for me;
> And from my smitten heart with tears
> Two wonders I confess—
> The wonders of His glorious love
> And my unworthiness.

It should not be hard to see one last picture in the Communion service. *We stand before an open tomb, rejoicing,* when we come to the altar for the Sacrament. For the Word who became flesh has conquered the terrible weaknesses of flesh—sin and death—and has triumphed over the power of darkness. That's why we can come to Holy Communion, believing that Christ gives us His body and His blood. If He had remained in the grave, this would be only an empty ceremony, a symbol, but nothing more. Some have reduced this ceremony to that level and have thus lost the Easter joy that is embodied in the service. But thank God, our Lord is risen and can come to us with His body and His blood, using the bread and the wine as channels. The Sacrament of the Altar is permeated with the story of Easter and the glad tidings of that day.

One of the most beautiful promises of the New Testament was given by Jesus when He appeared to Thomas after the resurrection. When the doubting one had confessed his faith, Jesus said, "Blessed are those who have not seen and yet believe," John 20:29. Isn't that our position when we come to Holy Communion? We have not seen our Lord face to face, nor can we fathom the mystery of the Sacrament and explain how Christ gives us His body and His blood. And yet we believe His Word. And so as we come to the altar we kneel beside a manger, we sup with the Master in an upper room, we gaze on His dying form on the cross, and we rejoice in His risen and living presence.

Lord Jesus Christ: We thank Thee that Thou didst take upon Thyself our human nature, and that through Thy sacrifice on the cross we have received power to become the children of God. We also give Thee thanks for the blessed gift of Thy body and Thy blood in Holy Communion. We do not deserve either Thy sacrifice or Thy gift. Yet help us, we pray Thee, to trust in Thy promises and to walk by faith through this dark world. Sustain us with Thy body and Thy blood until the day when we shall be with Thee in eternity. In Thy name we ask it all. Amen.

GIFTS UNSEEN BUT REAL

By Ross Stover

↗ ↗ ↗

Read John 6:41-59

"The cup of blessing which we bless, is it not a participation in the blood of Christ? The bread which we break, is it not a participation in the body of Christ?" I Corinthians 10:16.

↗

"I didn't see you at the Communion service," I said to a very conscientious Christian member of our church. After a pause and with humble attitude she replied: "I find that I am not good enough to commune. I am too much of a sinner."

That was, indeed, a shock to me because this lady had been a member of my church for many years. I certainly felt that my preaching had been inadequate. Immediately I sat down with her and began to explain again the very heart of the Communion which she was dreadfully missing.

I told her that to receive forgiveness was one of the very reasons for Christians partaking of the Holy Communion, and that if she would wait until she was "good enough" she would not kneel at Communion this side of heaven. She was missing the very heart of God's Word. So much of her religion had become humanized. Christianity is supernatural, miraculous. Man did not discover it. God revealed it from heaven. The revelation came from Him. She was growing weak in her "earthly religion" while a

74

heavenly Christianity with mighty power was awaiting ad-
mittance into her soul.

Ponder for a moment over the names of the Communion.
You will then see how supernatural it is. It is called "The
Lord's Supper," meaning that He has made the appointment. He has furnished it. We term it "The Table of the
Lord" with the thought that we are all His guests. He instituted it. He served the bread and the cup. "The Sacrament of the Altar" is familiar to us, which renders the
thought that it is God's sacrifice, complete and all-sufficient.
He gives to us the tremendous benefits. On our part it is
absolutely a reception, a serious but also a joyful reception.
Perhaps the most familiar name is "The Holy Communion,"
meaning communion with Jesus Christ, our Lord, that He
is truly received through the bread and the wine. The word
"Eucharist," while not used too often, conveys the lovely
thought that its reception is full of grace.

The heart is stirred by the first sentence uttered by our
Lord after they sat down at the table in the upper room.
Listen to it: "With desire have I desired to eat this passover with you before I suffer: For I say unto you, I will
not anymore eat thereof until it is fulfilled in the kingdom
of God," Luke 22:15, 16. The word "desire" is a revealing
word, fairly burning with the love of God for His children.
Down through the generations He has always fervently
desired our presence. He loves to have us with Him. He
desires to give us of His abundance.

And, my friend, please do not forget the fact that the
Holy Communion is a serious, satisfying, joyful banquet
which our Lord has instituted for you, His child. Certainly,
the first Communion in the upper room was sad. The disciples were fairly enshrouded in sorrow, thoughts of death,
and a feeling of defeat. They could not see through to the

victory as did Jesus. Think of it! When they arose from the table and started for the Garden of Gethsemane where He would be betrayed by one of His own, He said, "Be of good cheer, I have overcome the world." Our Holy Communion is alive, triumphant, full of the victorious Christ. The only touch of sadness would be when a communicant "remembers His death till He comes." However, even then we must remember the words of Scripture: "Yet it pleased the Lord to bruise Him," Isaiah 53:10.

"This Is My Body"

On that Holy Thursday night, known as "The Night of His Betrayal," Jesus sat in the midst of His disciples. After they had finished the Passover feast, He instituted the Lord's Supper. His words have both unified Christians throughout the ages and divided them into many interpretations. St. Matthew says: "Jesus took bread, and blessed it, and break it, and gave it to His disciples, and said: 'Take, eat, this is My body.' And He took the cup, and gave thanks, and gave it to them, saying, 'Drink ye all of it; for this is My blood of the new testament, which is shed for many for the remission of sins,'" Matthew 26:26-28. St. Mark records the institution in almost the same phraseology (Mark 14:22-25) while St. Luke adds, "This do in remembrance of Me." St. Paul, in First Corinthians 11:23-29, gives us a very full description of the institution of the Lord's Supper, adding the revealing word: "Body, which was broken for you." In verse 26 he tells us that the Lord's Supper is a proclamation that Jesus will come again: "For as often as ye eat this bread, and drink this cup, ye do show the Lord's death till He come." Indeed, when we kneel in Holy Communion we look to the past when it was instituted, to the future when all will be consummated, and to the present when we are receiving our Lord into our very being. In verse 27 Paul emphasizes the reception of the true body of Christ by the words: "Therefore whosoever shall eat this bread, and drink this cup of the Lord, unworthily, shall be guilty of the body and blood of the Lord." And in verse 29 a warning is given concerning the true presence of the body of Christ: "For he that eateth and drinketh unworthily, eateth and drinketh damnation to himself, not discerning the Lord's body." And, thanks to St. Paul, we have the interpretation of the reception of the body and the blood of Jesus in the Communion: "The cup of blessing which we bless, is it not the communion of the blood of Christ? The bread which we break, is it not the communion of the body of Christ?" I Corinthians 10:16.

The Roman Catholics believe that the bread and the wine change into the body and the blood of Christ: "This is My body. This is My blood." No longer is it bread or wine; even after the Communion they remain His body and His blood.

The Reformed Churches believe that the entire service is symbolic and a memorial, that the bread symbolizes the body of Christ, and the wine symbolizes the blood of Christ. They lay emphasis on "this do in remembrance of Me."

The Lutheran Church teaches that the bread and the wine do not change, but that the body and the blood of Christ are received by the communicant in, through, and under these elements. St. Paul's interpretation is our interpretation when he said: "The bread which we break, is it not a communion of the body of Christ?" He calls it "bread" while you are breaking it and consuming it. It never changes. It is a vehicle through which the body comes.

This miracle is not hard to believe in this day of radio, television, and radar. Atheists long ago laughed at the words: "In the last day, the trumpet shall sound," and, "Every eye shall see Him." How could one man in one place be seen? Or a trumpet in one place be heard? That sneering laughter has faded out with the miracles of radio and television. Naturally, we partake of the bread and the wine and sacramentally of His body and His blood. What a cathedral a believer becomes! On the other hand, without Christ we are like the unbeliever Renan whom a peasant in his day described as "like a cathedral which is no longer used for worship." With St. Paul we can say, "I live, yet not I, Christ liveth in me." In Holy Communion we receive a transfusion of the life of our Lord.

Before passing over this most important factor of the Communion I might state that one of the questions asked concerning Jesus, our Lord, giving us His true body and His blood in the Communion, is this: "How could Christ give the disciples His body when He was seated right there in their midst?" The Lord answered that question Himself when He said to Nicodemus: "Even the Son of man which is in heaven." As the second person in the triune God He was ruling over the universe while walking humbly on the earth.

"Hath Eternal Life"

God made us to live. Our business is living. Jesus said: "I am come that they might have life, and that they might have it more abundantly," John 10:10. When one is baptized, the seed of regeneration is planted in that life. It needs cultivating and culturing until the person believes on Jesus Christ as his personal Savior. When Jesus comes into the heart of the believer He brings eternal life. In the Holy Supper the faithful communicant receives eternal life in a very unique way. It is God's rich bestowal.

Jesus said: "I am the living bread that came down from heaven; if any man eat of this bread he shall live forever," John 6:51. We eat and live forever. With that devotion and loyalty we should prepare ourselves for the reception of the gift of eternal life. We must examine ourselves to be sure that we steadfastly believe; we must humbly confess our errors and our shortcomings; we must rid ourselves of every negative condition; then the room of the heart is big for our Lord to bestow life abundant.

We kneel at the altar, "remembering His death till He comes." We remember how He hung on the tree, His burial, His descent into hell, where He took death captive and conquered every fortress that would stand in the pathway of the believer. We remember Easter, how He arose from the grave. How He said: "Because I live ye shall live also." We remember how He said just before He ascended to the right hand of the Father: "Lo, I am with you always, even unto the end of the world." Remembering His exodus from the earth gives a Christian a sense of values. I love the words of Jesus: "He that believeth in Me shall never die." Eternal life, that is one of the major gifts in Holy Communion. All the undertakers in the world cannot bury your gift of eternal life.

> I came to Jesus, and I drank
> Of that life-giving stream.
> My thirst was quenched, my soul revived.
> And now I live in Him.

"Shed for You"

"This is My blood of the new testament which was shed for many for the remission of sins," Matthew 26:28. The Greek word for testament or covenant means will. By His death and His resurrection Christ probated it and sealed it. Now we are His heirs. And through the church God advertises for heirs in every generation. It is all summarized in that wonderful sentence: "As many as received Him to them gave He power to become the children of God."

The very heart of Christianity is forgiveness. It is one of the great factors which makes Christianity different from all other religions. Christ died for our sins. He was the Lamb slain on Calvary for the sins of the world. He became our substitute, taking our place. So they released the sinner Barabbas and killed Jesus. So we have been released from the prison of death and sin. He met the demands of justice. We sing it like this:

> Jesus paid it all, all to Him I owe:
> Sin had left a crimson stain,
> He washed it white as snow.

Look into the center of the channel of the grace of God and you will find the verse: "The blood of Jesus Christ, His Son, cleanseth us from all sin," I John 1:7. When you kneel at God's Holy Communion Table, remember that Christ drank the cup of sin to the very dregs. Now you come in faith, "remembering His death," claiming His sacrifice, and He bestows upon you the forgiveness of sins. You will never treat lightly that gift if you will look again and again at Calvary.

At the Communion Table you can lose all your sense and burden of guilt. Human psychology and psychiatry may show you ways of relief, but they play only on the fringes of what can occur at the altar in Holy Communion. To be forgiven is the need. Then guilt is removed. Then the joy of freedom in Christ is experienced. When we come remembering our sins, then He forgets them. At the altar we can say: "In my distress Thou hast enlarged my vision."

My friend, summarize the gifts of the Holy Communion, and you will readily see that the Lord's Supper is the most sacred place in the Christian's life. Never again will you come merely from custom. Never will you think of it as a rite rigidly to be observed as a law of the church. You will come with a heart filled with gratitude. You will gaze upon Him whom you are receiving. It will be a joyful reception. Here God will give you a blank check to be filled in by your faith. No sweeter words will have ever fallen on your ears than the benediction chosen for this marvelous occasion:

> "The body of our Lord Jesus Christ
> and His precious blood strengthen and
> preserve you in true faith
> unto everlasting life."

Our heavenly Father: We look up to Thee in adoration and in love. Thou hast loved us with an everlasting love. May we continually experience Thy wondrous compassion as we humbly kneel before Thee.

We are Thy children. Our greatest privilege is to live our life, knowing that we are in the presence of our loving God. At this moment we confess our sins to Thee, realizing that we have missed the mark; we have fallen short of our high calling. We ask that Thou wilt forgive us our trespasses, not that we are worthy, but in the mighty name of Thy Son, Jesus Christ, and for the sake of His precious blood shed for us.

Abide with us this day so that we may better do Thy will. Guide Thy church throughout the world that faithful ministers and laymen may share the gospel with those in darkness and in need.

Use us this day, dear Lord, to further Thy cause and the kingdom of heaven. And may we so realize that "the joy of the Lord is our strength," that our witness for Thee will be optimistic and victorious.

We pray in the blessed name of Jesus Christ. Amen.

THE MAGNETISM OF THE CROSS

By P. O. Bersell

⸕ ⸕ ⸕

Read John 12:27-32

"I, when I am lifted up from the earth, will draw all men to Myself," John 12:32.

⸕

This meditation is for sinners only. To those who deem themselves righteous the crucified Savior has no significance. They have no need of Him.

Recently one of America's most distinguished citizens died. His office was second in honor and responsibility only to that of the president. I was truly startled when I read this published paragraph from his last will and testament: "I pass from the stage of life with no regrets so far as wrong-doing is concerned. I confide my soul to my Maker's care in the firm belief that He will pronounce me pure of heart and entitled by my life and love and respect for Him to partake of the reward which He has awaiting us."

How pathetic, how tragic! For this man had at least been exposed to the teachings of the Christian gospel. Is this a typical example of the contemporary American faith, the result of modern, popular preaching? Do a lot of folks, allegedly Christian, really believe that they can "lift themselves to heaven by their own bootstraps"?

In sharp contrast with this we hear the truth as proclaimed in God's Holy Word. The angel of God proclaimed, "His name shall be called Jesus, for He shall save His people from their sins." The Savior said, "No man comes to the Father except by Me." And in that remarkable third chapter of the letter to the Romans we read: "None is righteous, no not one, no one does good, no not one. All men are under the power of sin. No human being will be justified in God's sight by works of the law, for all have sinned and fall short of the glory of God—they are justified by His grace, as a gift, through the redemption which is in Christ Jesus."

This, then, is the real meaning of the words of Jesus, "When I am lifted up from the earth, I will draw all men to Myself." For immediately following this saying in Holy Writ comes the explanation, "He said this to show by what death He was to die."

This is the magnetism of the cross, the drawing power of the crucified Savior. But does He really mean that "all men" will be drawn to Him and be saved?

God created man in His own image, with a free will. And even when man fell into sin and turned his back on God, He did not take away from him his free will. He still has the power to say no to God. No one is forced into the kingdom of heaven. God calls and entreats, all too often in vain. For all that, the magnetism of the cross is still the greatest, the most benign power in all the world. It is so great that it is hard to understand how anyone can resist it, once exposed to it.

What, then, is the magnetic power of the cross? It is the love of God, demonstrated in the supreme sacrifice of His only-begotten Son, in and through whose atoning death and victorious resurrection that love was translated into the saving grace of God in Christ Jesus, the redemption through His blood. It is the abiding presence of Christ in Word and Sacrament. "When I am lifted up," said Jesus, and there can be no doubt that He had in mind not only the crucifixion, for He was not to remain on the cross, but also His ascension into heaven, in both His divine and human nature, to sit in glory on the right hand of the Father, to rule as King in the kingdom of grace. It is this same, complete, ever-present Savior who invites us to His Supper, and, therefore, we can believe in His real presence in the Sacrament according to His own word.

And what is the purpose of this drawing? It is to give to sinners that which they need most of all, the forgiveness of sins. That is the great calling and mission of the church in this world, to proclaim to sinners the forgiveness of sins. For when sin is forgiven and conquered, there follow peace and joy and the power of the life in God. We experience then the truth of the words which our eyes have read and our lips have repeated over and over again, even from our childhood, that "where there is forgiveness of sin, there is also life and salvation." God's objective in Christ for us is that we may again become and remain His children, His very own, to live under Him in His kingdom and serve Him in everlasting righteousness, innocence, and blessedness.

Why is it that all do not come, that seemingly the great majority is immune to the magnetism of the cross? In the physical world it is true that the magnet, no matter how powerful it may be, cannot attract all to itself. For there may be other forces and attachments that hinder and hold. So in human life and in the spiritual world there are also other magnets, other attractions that hinder and nullify the magnetism of the cross on the human heart. We mention but a few of these. There is, first of all, pride. Some folks feel they have nothing to repent of. Or if they are conscious of some sins or weaknesses they readily find excuses for them or are confident in their own ability ultimately to conquer them.

Then there is the bondage of sin which grips like a vise. It may be the lusts of the flesh. It may be a secret, shameful sin that enslaves. Or it may be selfishness or avarice or just the love of the present world that neutralizes the magnetism of the cross. Again it may be fear. One will say: "I am too great a sinner. I cannot be forgiven." And another will say: "My faith is not strong enough. I cannot be accepted."

The loving patience of Christ is beyond our comprehension. In spite of rebuffs He continues to invite. In spite of the seeming imperviousness of the human heart He continues to draw. If this were not true, very few would be saved. God be praised for His long-suffering!

Would that all sinners, under conviction of sin, might believe the Word of God, "It is a faithful saying and worthy of all acceptation that Jesus Christ came into the world to save sinners," and again, "The blood of Jesus, God's Son, cleanses from all sin." Let him who trembles in his weakness of faith cry out: "Lord, I believe. Help my unbelief."

For our acceptance of Christ does not depend on the strength of our faith but rather on the realization of our utter need of Him and His saving grace and on the sincerity of our heart as we respond to His call. The test of our faith is its genuineness.

Today the Savior invites us to His table. The uplifted One, whose body was nailed to, and whose blood was shed upon the cross, draws us with His gracious call. "Come," He says, "take, eat; this is My body. Drink, this is My blood of the covenant, which is poured out for many for the forgiveness of sins." Christ offers Himself to us in the fulness of His redeeming, saving grace.

This is, indeed, a divine miracle. It doesn't take much faith to accept the bread and the wine as mere symbols or to partake of the Holy Supper as a memorial feast. But here is something infinitely greater. Faith is "the conviction of things not seen." Such a faith rests upon the Word of

God. And He, "the Word become flesh," says, "This is My body—this is My blood." Faith does not discount even if it cannot explain. Human language cannot improve upon the words of Jesus. We say that "in, with, and under the bread and the wine, consecrated by the divine words of institution, we receive the true body and blood of Christ." Or we say that "the earthly elements are the vehicles by which Christ transmits to us Himself." But the original words stand in all their marvelous simplicity, "This is My body—this is My blood—for the forgiveness of sins." These words are the proclamation of, and the guarantee of, the real presence of our Lord in His Holy Supper.

What an invitation to sinners who need forgiveness! What a glad proclamation to those who are burdened with guilt, and who know that they can do nothing in and of themselves to become free! We cannot even believe in Jesus Christ by our own reason or strength or come to Him. But the Holy Spirit calls, enlightens, liberates, and we yield ourselves to the magnetism of the cross. Then is our sin forgiven, and the Son makes us free, and the joy of salvation is ours.

It is no wonder that of old the Sacrament of the Altar was called the Eucharist, the festival of thanksgiving. God be praised for this blessed feast! With gladness let us come as penitent sinners to enjoy this foretaste of heaven to the joy of our soul and the strengthening of our faith.

Our God and Father, may we, by Thy grace, be ever grateful for the body and the blood of our Savior as Thou hast seen fit to grant them to us in the Sacrament. Cause us to rejoice in the Lord, our Savior, and live our life in such a manner that His name may be glorified and His kingdom increased. We pray in His holy name. Amen.

DISCERNING THE LORD'S BODY

By Robert H. Boyd

✦ ✦ ✦

Read John 6:25-58

"Whoever, therefore, eats the bread or drinks the cup of the Lord in an unworthy manner will be guilty of profaning the body and the blood of the Lord. Let a man examine himself, and so eat of the bread and drink of the cup. For anyone who eats and drinks without discerning the body eats and drinks judgment on himself," I Corinthians 11:27-29.

✦

"My conscience is captive to God's Word." In these words Martin Luther gave his answer to the demand that he repudiate all his reformatory writings. "My conscience is captive to God's Word. I cannot and I will not recant anything. For to go against conscience is neither right nor safe. God help me. Here I stand. I cannot do otherwise." The place was the Diet of Worms. The event—one of the most dramatic in history. Many see in it the beginning of modern times.

As followers of the great reformer we, too, would place our conscience under the captivity of God's Word. We, therefore, insist that all our doctrine must stem from the Word alone.

One of the most crucial doctrines, the one which separates us most decisively from other Christian denominations and sects, is our teaching regarding the real presence of Christ in the Lord's Supper. We believe that our view is the one that Scripture teaches.

What is the Sacrament of the Altar? "It is [as Luther states in his Small Catechism] the true body and blood of our Lord Jesus Christ, under the bread and wine, given unto us Christians to eat and to drink, as it was instituted by Christ Himself."

Without any attempt to explain how it is possible for Christ to be truly present in the Lord's Supper we as Lutherans simply take His words at their face value when He declares concerning the bread and the wine: "This is My body. . . . This is My blood of the covenant which is poured out for many for the forgiveness of sins," Matthew 26:26, 28.

Why do we hold to this doctrine, all logic and reason to the contrary? It is because the Scriptures affirm so positively the real presence. With Luther we, therefore, declare: "Our conscience is bound in God's Word."

There is no Scripture passage dealing with the Lord's Supper that implies that His declaration should be taken in a figurative, symbolic, or even merely spiritual sense. As Prof. Werner Elert puts it: "The Lord's Supper looms up like a towering rock even in the very oldest documents of Christianity . . . . It is incapable of further development and requires none. It mocks every attempt to spiritualize it."[1]

The three Synoptic Gospels unanimously agree that our Lord stated concerning the bread and the wine: "This is My body . . . . This is My blood." None of them implies that He meant thereby: "This symbolizes My body . . . This symbolizes My blood." If our Lord had meant this He

---

1. Werner Elert, *Morphologie des Luthertums,* C. H. Bech'sche Verlagsbuchhandlung, Muenchen, (1931), I, p. 280. Used by permission of the publisher.

would have expressed Himself more clearly, especially at such a critical moment, when He was soon to leave His disciples to go to the cross. He would have qualified His words by some further explanation. It is likely that at least one of the evangelists would have added a word of explanation as St. John does to the statement of Jesus in John 12:32: "And I, when I am lifted up from the earth, will draw all men to Myself." In verse 33 he adds: "He said this to show by what death He was to die." Nowhere in the record, however, is there a statement qualifying Jesus' words in order to make them more understandable.

St. Paul's description of the Lord's Supper in First Corinthians indicates that he did not hold the view that Jesus was using only symbolic language. In fact, his statement, "Anyone who eats and drinks without discerning the body eats and drinks judgment upon himself," shows that he did believe that we actually receive the body of Christ in the Sacrament. Previously he had directed these questions to his readers: "The cup of blessing which we bless, is it not a participation in the blood of Christ? The bread which we break, is it not a participation in the body of Christ?" I Corinthians 10:16, 17. Accordingly Prof. Herbert T. Andrews, prominent British New Testament scholar, after a careful study of all the pertinent passages in St. Paul declares: "It becomes very doubtful whether any theory that falls short of the Lutheran doctrine of consubstantiation will adequately explain the utterance of St. Paul in reference to the Eucharist."[2] The late Dr. Andrews was not himself a Lutheran.

---

2. "The Place of the Sacraments in the Teaching of St. Paul," chapter 8, p. 163, in P. T. Forsyth, *The Church and the Sacraments*. 3d ed. London (1949). Used by permissiin of the publisher, Independent Press.

We as Lutherans appreciate his testimony to the ex-
egetical soundness of our doctrine concerning the real presence although we would repudiate his description of the
Lutheran view as consubstantiation. Our confessions and
our dogmaticians have clearly rejected this term, which
implies a local presence of the body and the blood of Christ
in the bread and the wine, a co-mingling of the bread and
the wine with the body and the blood of Christ so that they
form one conglomerate substance.[3]

What, then, is the meaning of our teaching concerning
the real presence of Christ in the Sacrament? It is easier to
describe what it is not than to describe what it is.

We do not mean the Roman view, that bread and wine
are miraculously changed into the body and the blood of
Christ when the priest celebrates the Mass. This miracle
theory, transubstantiation as it is called, did not become
the official doctrine of the Roman Church until the thirteenth century A. D. About this time the church began to
withhold the wine from the laity because it was maintained
that the bread which had become Christ's flesh would con-
tain some blood anyway. The laity was not permitted to
drink of the cup for fear some of the precious blood of
Christ might be spilled. When the light of Scripture shone
into the heart of Luther, he repudiated this theory and
declared that the bread remained bread, and the wine remained wine, but that the body and the blood of Christ
were present in a sacramental, supernatural manner for
every communicant.

He refused, however, to go along with the Swiss reformer Zwingli, who declared that the bread and the wine
were merely symbolical representatives of Christ's body
and His blood—nothing more. At the famous colloquy of

3. Krauth, C. P., *The Conservative Reformation and its Theology.*
Philadelphia (1871), pp. 339-341.

Marburg in October, 1529, when the two men met with other Protestant reformers to draw up a common confession of faith, he refused to admit any kind of symbolic or figurative interpretation of Jesus' words. He drew a circle with chalk upon the table and wrote within it our Lord's words, "This is My body!" When Zwingli declared that the flesh and the spirit are incompatible, and that Christ's presence in the Sacrament could, therefore, be at most only spiritual, Luther replied that flesh and spirit can be conjoined. In Christ we see God becoming man. God is as truly present in the Sacrament as He was born of the Virgin. To Luther there was a close relationship between the incarnation of Christ and His real presence in the Sacrament.

When with Luther we insist that Christ is not present in a merely spiritual manner but in a direct personal way we do not deny that He is not also present in a spiritual manner in the Sacrament. Whenever we hear the gospel of Christ and trustfully receive it into our heart we partake of Him spiritually as the bread of life. In the Lord's Supper we hear His Word and have opportunity to meditate upon it. As we listen to it in faith, appropriate it to ourselves, and firmly rely on it, we do spiritually eat the body of Christ and drink His blood. This is the kind of eating Jesus talks about in John 6:25-58.

But we insist that Jesus' declaration at the time He instituted the Lord's Supper indicates that He comes to us also in a direct and personal way in the Sacrament. To emphasize this fact Luther uses the expression "in, with, and under the bread and wine." Such language, however, does not imply that Christ is present in a carnal, physical manner so that we actually eat part of His flesh and drink part of His blood. All our confessions as well as Luther himself clearly repudiate any teaching that implies a localized presence of the body and the blood in the bread and the wine. Our Lord is present, not in a fleshly manner perceivable to the senses, but in a supernatural manner that we shall never be able to comprehend. We believe He is present, however, not because we can explain His presence, but because He says so.

Abraham likewise took God at His word when he was asked to offer up his son Isaac, the very child through whom God had declared Abraham would have many descendants. Abraham did not say to himself: "Perhaps God does not really require me to offer Isaac. Maybe He only intends that I offer him in symbolic fashion." No, Abraham gave God the honor of truth, trusting that what He had promised He would do although it appeared impossible to his reason.

We cannot understand how Christ can be present in the Sacrament. Yet this should not cause us to deny that He can be present in the Lord's Supper and still be seated at the throne of God in heaven. By radio and television we experience the presence of individuals every day though they remain in the studio from whence their broadcast or telecast comes. Who of our grandparents would have believed that a man could stand in New York and speak in an ordinary voice and at the same moment be seen and heard in thousands of homes throughout the land without in any way diminishing his presence? We know now, however, that it is possible.

This is not intended to be an analogy for the real presence of Christ in the Sacrament. There is no analogy adequate to explain it, for the manner of His presence is supernatural, beyond our power to comprehend. The minor matter, after all, is the "how" of His presence; the major matter is to *recognize* His presence in holy and saving action.

It is because our Lord is truly present in the bread and the wine of the Sacrament that we can be sure that it bestows a blessing that no other feast does. Through this feast Christ gives Himself anew to us, the gift of His forgiveness and His reconciliation which He made possible once for all by His death upon the cross. As we kneel at His altar we are baptized into His death, and we assimilate it as a real death that took place for us. It is the real Christ that enters us, the same Lord who as flesh and blood walked the earth and by His triumphant redemption gives us eternal life. This is the blessing which all those who believe receive. This same feast, however, becomes a curse to those who disbelieve. "Whoever eats the bread or drinks the cup of the Lord in an unworthy manner will be guilty of profaning the body and blood of the Lord," I Corinthians 11:27.

How important, therefore, that we examine our heart as we eat the bread and drink the cup so that we may approach His table in a worthy, that is, believing manner.

> O God, unseen yet ever near,
> Thy presence may we feel;
> And thus, inspired with holy fear,
> Before Thine altar kneel.
>
> We come, obedient to Thy word,
> To feast on heavenly food:
> Our meat, the body of the Lord;
> Our drink, His precious blood.
>
> Thus would we all Thy words obey.
> For we, O God, are Thine;
> And go rejoicing on our way,
> Renewed with strength divine.
>
> —*E. Osler.*

IN REMEMBRANCE OF ME

By O. P. Kretzmann

↗ ↗ ↗

Read Acts 2:37-47

"This do in remembrance of Me," Luke 22:19b.

↗

It is Sunday morning in a thousand Lutheran churches throughout the land. The sermon has ended. The congregation rises for the Offertory. Once more the ancient, beautiful words rise through the church to the altar: "Create in me a clean heart . . . Renew a right spirit within me . . . . Cast me not away from Thy presence . . . . Restore unto me the joy of Thy salvation." The last sentence is particularly significant. In a day when our Christian faith is so often identified with darkness and gloom it is good for us to remember every Sunday that our faith is a great, joyous, and happy thing. The joy of Thy salvation! This is the secret of the Christian life. This is the great heart of the truly Christian relationship to God and to man.

The pastor descends from the pulpit and announces the hymn preceding the celebration of Holy Communion. In many churches it undoubtedly is the magnificent, joyful chorale:

> "Soul, adorn thyself with gladness,
> Leave behind all gloom and sadness;
> Come into the daylight's splendor,
> There with joy thy praises render

94

Unto Him whose grace unbounded
Hath this wondrous Supper founded.
High o'er all the heav'ns He reigneth,
Yet to dwell with thee He deigneth."

Again there is the same singing, soaring note of joy and gladness. A great moment in the Christian life is approaching. A moment of deep happiness and lasting joy!

The pastor moves to the altar and reverently prepares the vessels for the Lord's Supper. He turns to the congregation, and the age-old liturgy begins: "The Lord be with you; And with thy spirit." As at the very beginning of the entire service, the pastor and the people once more bespeak for each other the full and abiding presence of the living God. There is a brief preface or foreword which identifies the season of the church year in which this particular service is being conducted. Immediately after that there is again the note of grateful joy: "With angels and archangels and all the company of heaven we laud and magnify Thy glorious name," the Lord's Prayer, and then the solemn words of institution, the consecration of the bread and the wine with the searching words, "In remembrance of Me."

These words indicate clearly the first purpose of the Supper instituted by our Lord on the night before His death. In remembrance of Me! Through the silence of the long centuries comes the haunting, pleading voice, "This do in remembrance of Me." At this point the Lutheran Christian at the Communion service preparing for the Lord's Supper must be very sure of the meaning of these words. Perhaps we can remember the beautiful explanation of Martin Luther in our Small Catechism. "What ought we to do when we eat His body and drink His bood and thus receive the pledge?" Answer: "We ought to proclaim His death and the shedding of His blood as He taught us: This do as oft as ye drink it, in remembrance of Me."

"Why ought we to remember and proclaim His death?"

"That we may learn to believe that no creature could make satisfaction for our sins but Christ through God and man, and that we may learn to look with terror at our sins and to regard them as great indeed and to find joy and comfort in Him alone, and thus be saved through such faith."

This is the very center of the Christian faith. It draws us up the hill of Calvary and into the shadow of the cross. We can never forget that the source of all power and joy in the Christian life lies at the foot of the cross. Who comes to us in the Lord's Supper? The Christ of the cross, the Lamb of the eternal sacrifice, the sin-burdened fashioner of atonement. Once more we see the silences of eternity, the counsels of the Holy Trinity, the crying of prophets, the long nights of waiting, the voice of a Child in a manger, Palm Sunday, Easter, Ascension, and Pentecost, all point to the center of the world's history and the heart of the world's hope—the cross of Jesus Christ. Here the conflict of sin and grace comes to a burning focus. Here we see the full generosity of God and the full shame of man. This is what He meant when He said: "In remembrance of Me."

As always in the shadow of the cross, life and history and time become clear and sharp. Here, as Luther indicates, we see two things: first, the terror of sin; and, second, the joy of salvation. Among the many tragically wrong things in the modern world none is more saddening than our frequent misunderstanding of the word "sin." We are in danger of forgetting that our Lutheran doctrine of justification by faith always presupposes a deep, God-given consciousness of sin. This was the way of St. Paul, St. Augustine, and Martin Luther. All of them felt the terror of sin like the lash of a whip. They felt sin in the one way in which the modern mind does not feel it, namely, as the real reason for our broken world.

It is only at the foot of the cross and in the God-given remembrance of our Savior that we realize that sin is always the breaking down of fellowship. The ruin is more complete the higher we go. Every reference to sin in Holy Writ always pictures it as wandering, loneliness, going away, going astray, separation. It is always the same tolling theme. We had a home once, and we lost it. We had a fellowship, and we broke it. We had a love, and we forgot it.

As we confess our sins and receive the absolution, this must be uppermost in our mind. We must realize how great our distance from God has been, and how deeply and bitterly we need our Savior's body and His blood for the assurance of release from the terror and the horror of sin.

The words of institution have been spoken, the Agnus Dei has been sung, and the Communion begins. Silently and reverently the worshipers approach the altar. Just what is happening there now? Again there is no better answer than the simple, clear words of Martin Luther's Small Catechism. "You believe, then, that the true body and blood of Christ are in the Sacrament?"

"Yes, I believe it."

"What induces you to believe this?"

"The Word of Christ: 'Take, eat, this is My body; drink ye all of it, this is My blood.'"

In God's own mysterious way the simple bread and wine become truly the body and the blood of the Savior of the world. In, with, and under these signs there is the real presence of the God-man Jesus Christ.

It is this real presence of our Savior in the Sacrament which gives it its tremendous spiritual power. Through the

bread and the wine He comes to us with the great and absolute assurance of the forgiveness of our sins. In the Lord's
Supper we are face to face with the amazing miracle of
God's love, the restoration of fellowship, the return to the
Father's house. In our Savior our brokenness is healed, and
our union with God and man is restored. The great separation now, so long and so bitter, has been ended by our
reunion with God through the work of Jesus Christ. The
bonds of sin are loosed. We have again the freedoms beneath and beyond all human freedoms—the freedom from
fear of sin, the freedom from want of God, the freedom of
worship of God, the freedom of speech to God. All this
comes to us in the Word and the sacraments by the full,
free grace of God.

It is necessary always to remember that the forgiveness
of our sins, the message of the Christian gospel, is the story
of an accomplished fact. We are face to face in the Sacrament with a finished redemption. One of the most curious
things in church history is the desire of men to return to
the paganism of the law. All about us we see the effort to
make Christianity a quest instead of an achievement. Over
against that our Lord's institution of the Lord's Supper
makes it perfectly clear for all time that the work of the
forgiveness of our sins is complete by any and every standard of measurement, human or divine. In the Word and
in the Sacrament He assures that He has restored the divine
balance between justice and mercy. Now and forever mercy
rules in His church.

This, then, is the reason for the joy of our salvation. In
the Sacrament we are again united with the suffering Christ,
the risen Christ, the conquering Christ of the past. In the
Sacrament we are united with the waiting and mediating
Christ of the present and the future. In remembrance of

Him we remember, too, that He is now in the majestic stillness of eternity, waiting for history to accomplish His last purposes. Through the centuries He sends the Comforter, perpetually hears our prayers and praises, and waits for us to reach the end of our journey and come home to His home in our own evening time. As we remember Him in the Sacrament, so He remembers us as our great Mediator.

This great remembrance should come more frequently to all true believers. The regular use of the means of grace is the greatest guarantee of joy in our soul and peace in our heart. Remembering Him we can also remember His words on the night of the beginning of the Lord's Supper: "Fear not; I have overcome the world."

Dear God, Thou who art forever God and Lord, we are grateful for the church, for Thy faithful ministers, and above all for Thy Word and sacraments. We do not ask that the divine mystery of the body and the blood be explained to our finite mind, we ask only that we may receive the blessed assurance, the wondrous hope, and the great joy which are ours because Thou didst give Thine only-begotten Son as a free gift to benighted mankind. Mindful of the treasure which is ours, we do thank and praise Thy precious name! Amen.

A JOYFUL RECEPTION

By Conrad Bergendoff

↙ ↙ ↙

Read Ephesians 3:14-21

"This is My body . . . This is My blood," Mark 14:22, 24.

↙

These are the words with which I receive the bread and the wine at the Lord's Table. These are the words that the Savior spoke as He gave the bread and the cup to the disciples who were with Him at the first Communion. Without these words there would be but bread and wine at the altar before which I kneel. But with these words the bread and the wine become a sacrament. They are themselves a gift of God for which I can give thanks. But a sacrament is more than a gift of bread and wine. A sacrament is a token of the presence of God Himself.

That the body and the blood of Christ are given with the bread and the wine has led some to think that by some magical process the bread and the wine are changed into something else than what they naturally are. But there is no such teaching in the New Testament. The bread remains bread, the wine remains wine. They are like any other bread and wine. We do speak of consecrated bread and wine, that is, this bread and this wine are set aside for the purpose of Communion. But this effects no change in them. After the Communion, if there should be bread remaining or wine, it is still bread and wine. So it is not in the bread or the wine that the sacrament consists. The sacrament is in the Word which is associated with this particular use of bread and wine.

It was in the night in which He was betrayed that Jesus instituted this sacrament. He had withdrawn from the crowds that followed Him and the enemies who soon would capture Him. Together with His own disciples He had wanted to eat the Passover meal in quiet, before the events He knew awaited Him. The Passover was in His mind as well as in the mind of all who celebrated this feast. It recalled the night when Israel left Egypt (Exodus 12). The night an angel of the Lord smote the first-born in every home except where the Passover sign of blood was on the doorway. It was a night of death and a night of deliverance. The people of God were to be saved from their oppressor. They were to go forth to live as God's people.

In that night, when Jesus knew one of His disciples was to betray Him, He gathered His own around Him. He knew that He would be crucified. But He also knew that it was for this purpose He came to earth. He came to bear the sins of the world so that the children of God might escape the death those sins brought on them. As in ancient Egypt the lamb was slain whose blood was to be the sign of the passing by of the angel of death, so Christ had come to be a Lamb sacrificed for the sins of the world. Those who were in His company were to be saved. With Him they would pass out of the bondage of sin and live in the fellowship of the people of God.

In the Gospel of John there is a series of chapters (13-17) in which the evangelist tells us of the words and the prayer of Jesus in that night. With His disciples around Him He foretells what is to happen, how He will leave them, but how He will send the Holy Spirit to teach and to aid them. He prays that those who believe in Him may all be one, united with Him as the branches of the vine are one with the vine. And He asks, "Father, I will that they also, whom Thou hast given Me, be with Me where I am; that they may behold My glory, which Thou hast given Me," John 17:24.

Luke tells us that Jesus added the words, "This do in remembrance of Me" as He gave them the cup, and Paul, in writing to the Corinthians, also reports Jesus' words, "This do in remembrance of Me," I Corinthians 11:24, 25. We know that the celebration of the Sacrament became a regular observance of the disciples after His resurrection and has continued through two thousand years to be the central act of Christian worship. Still today the liturgy of the Sacrament contains the words of institution as the foundation of our belief that Christ is truly present with His people as they "do this in remembrance" of Him.

Each time that we hear these words, "This is My body . . . . This is My blood," and receive the bread and the wine we are as the disciples around their present Savior. We believe that He comes again to us through all the barriers of distance in time and space and is in our midst. He grants us in this Sacrament the assurance of His having come to earth, of His death for our sins, of His resurrection, and of eternal life.

Of course, there is a sense in which the Son of God is everywhere present. He through whom all things are made, as John says of Him (John 1:3), and He whose fulness "filleth all in all," as Paul declares (Ephesians 1:23), may be said to be in all places. But *we* do not see Him everywhere present. It is for our sake that He prepares a table for us where we may meet Him.

On the evening of His resurrection two disciples were walking from Jerusalem to the suburb of Emmaus. They were engaged in conversation concerning the things which had happened on the Friday of Jesus' death. A stranger joined their company and went with them to their destination. And, we read in Luke: "It came to pass, as He sat at meat with them, He took bread, and blessed it, and brake, and gave to them. And their eyes were opened, and they knew Him," Luke 24:31. The supper at Emmaus illustrates how in the breaking of bread the risen Christ was present.

And we need to recall that, when the disciples repeated the words of institution as they gathered for worship, doing this in remembrance of Him in the night in which He was betrayed, they celebrated the Sacrament, not as a memorial to one who was dead, but in the firm belief that He was risen from the dead and present among them. Also in the letter to the Corinthians Paul speaks of the church as the body of Christ. As Jesus had said He was the vine in which the branches had their life, so Paul says that Christ is the body in which all the members live, "For as the body is one, and hath many members, and all the members of that one body, are one body: so also is Christ. For by one Spirit are we all baptized into one body . . . . Now ye are the body of Christ," I Corinthians 12:12, 13, 27. And all through the New Testament Christians are represented as living "in Christ," in the body of Christ, the risen one.

The New Testament Church is the body of the risen Christ into whom the members are brought by baptism, and in whom they live by faith. When the congregation celebrates the Eucharist or Thanksgiving, it is a meeting again of the risen Christ with His people. This is the true fulfilment of the promise, "Where two or three are gathered together in My name, there am I in the midst of you," Matthew 18:20, for to be together in His name is to be where He has made an appointment with us. It is as if He should say, "Behold, I am with you alway," but whenever you come

together to eat the bread and drink the wine of the Supper
there My body and blood will be—there you will see Me
in the only form you may see Me on earth. I came to earth
and became incarnate in flesh and blood. This body was
broken, this blood was shed, for your sins. By baptism you
were buried with Me in My body into death (Romans 6:4).
But you were raised with Me from the dead so that you
might live with Me. "The cup of blessing which we bless is it
not the communion of the blood of Christ? The bread which
we break, is it not the communion of the body of Christ?"
I Corinthians 10:16. Our meeting with Christ at the Table is
a reaffirmation of our being "planted together" with Him
(Romans 6:5), our belonging to Him with whom "I am crucified—so that not I, but Christ liveth in me," Galatians 2:20.

When we speak, therefore, of the presence of Christ in
the Sacrament we confess our faith that He is risen, that
He is ascended, but that, true to His word, His body and
His blood are with those who in remembrance of Him
"show the Lord's death till He come," I Corinthians 11:26.
Just as He showed the wounds in His body to the doubting
Thomas after He had come through closed doors to the
company of disciples, so in the Sacrament the broken bread
and the cup of wine reveal to us Him who dies on the cross
for our sins but is risen from the grave for our righteousness.
He speaks to us the word of forgiveness which removes the
load of guilt and sin none else could take from us. He speaks
the word of peace which the world cannot give but is the
peace of the God of all grace and life.

That He should make this the supreme revelation of
His presence in His church on earth has always mystified
those who are blind to His appearance. They would suppose
the Creator of heaven and earth, the Lord of lords and King
of kings, to come with splendor and glory. But they have

never understood, indeed, His own disciples have had difficulty in understanding, the revelation of His glory which He also gave in the night He was betrayed. John gives us the record: "Jesus knowing that the Father had given all things into His hands, and that He was come from God, and went to God, riseth from the supper, and laid aside His garments; and took a towel, and girded Himself. After that He poured water into a basin, and began to wash the disciples' feet, and to wipe them with the towel wherewith He was girded," John 13:3-5.

If we would but ponder that act on the part of Him who then could say to the Father, "I have glorified Thee on earth," John 17:4, we might revise our notions of glory and begin to understand the glory of the love of God. Then, too, we might find it easier to understand the glory of the Sacrament and to believe that He who sits on the right hand of the Father is also present with His body and His blood to those who in faith receive the bread and the wine in remembrance of Him. Humbly and gratefully we would receive His promise, "He that eateth My flesh, and drinketh My blood, dwelleth in Me, and I in him," John 6:56.

Lord Jesus, humbly and joyfully I hear Thy word: "This is My body—given for you. This is My blood—shed for you." For me Thou hast come to earth and given Thy life upon the cross. For me Thou hast risen from the grave that I might live. For me Thou comest in Word and in Sacrament. Take me as I am. Create within me a clean heart. Renew within me a right spirit. Restore unto me the joy of Thy salvation. Thou livest—I shall live. Thou upholdest and guidest me. Let me follow Thee until with Thy loved ones I may be numbered at the heavenly altar. Unite here and finally there all Thy church in one body and one spirit. Come, O Lord Jesus. Amen.

REJOICE, MY SOUL!

By Gustav J. Neumann

𝄪 𝄪 𝄪

Read Psalm 121

"Then said Jesus unto them, Verily, verily, I say unto you, Except ye eat the flesh of the Son of man, and drink His blood, ye have no life in you.

"Whoso eateth My flesh, and drinketh My blood, hath eternal life; and I will raise him up at the last day.

"For My flesh is meat indeed, and My blood is drink indeed.

"He that eateth My flesh, and drinketh My blood, dwelleth in Me and I in him.

"As the living Father hath sent Me, and I live by the Father: so he that eateth Me, even he shall live by Me.

"This is that bread which came down from heaven: not as your fathers did eat manna, and are dead: he that eateth of this bread shall live for ever," John 6:53-56.

𝄪

How lovingly gracious the merciful Father in heaven has shown Himself to body and soul of this wayward me! For surely it was for me, blind and astray in the world's labyrinthine ways, it was for me and for my salvation that the Father, throned above the seraphim in power and majesty, suffered his only-begotten Son to humble Himself, to be born of Mary in the dim stall and be laid in a manger mean, fellowed by ox and ass. It was for me that, homeless, maligned, threatened, and opposed, the Prince of glory wandered up and down the flinty roads, crying the good news of God's grace and the coming of the kingdom. It was for me that He suffered Himself to be betrayed under the olives and by one of His twelve; to be made a mockery by His own creation, spat upon, smitten, and crowned with thorns; to be driven up the dolorous way, panting and stumbling under the weight of the shameful wood; to be nailed to the cursed tree and to be lifted up between the malefactors. It was for me that he bore the piercing agony of death. For me, for me, for me—in order that I might be His own, walk in the knowledge of His loving care through the dark gates of death, and with confidence enter into the timeless congregation of saints and angels about His shining throne. Oh, rejoice, my soul, and be glad within me!

And rejoice, rejoice, my soul, that God in His mercy has opened my eyes to the abundance of His grace and the blessed way of salvation! Oh, what a treasure I have in His Holy Word! Day by day His servants, inspired, emboldened, and made glad by the Holy Spirit, in these sacred pages invite me to hear and to hear again the wondrous chronicle of God's saving grace. What golden prophecies and what glorious fulfillments! With Adam and Eve am I dispossessed of Eden, but a greater Adam has opened the gates again. Through the washing of regeneration I am again a child of God; I am again God's very own. He watches over me throughout the days and seasons and through all the years of my life. My rising and my lying down are in His hands; my going and my coming are in His tender care. Am I in sore need of guidance? How willing and able He is to grant it in answer to my lifted prayer! Do I want strength for the heavenward march? Ah, but He, and He alone, is the everflowing fountain and source! Am I cast down? See how His

heart and His bosom yearn for me—His is the arm that
tenderly lifts me up, His are the lips that tenderly comfort
me, His is the hand that tenderly dries my tears. Does my
zeal wane? He calls me by name and directs my vision to
the hills everlasting and to the city not made of hands. Rejoice, my soul, for I am surely His! If I but wholly place
me in His care, there can no evil befall this child of God's.

I am God's child, for He has called me through His
Word, and He has made me His own by the holy cleansing
of His baptism. I am His, and He is mine. For God has
not only given Himself *for* me through the Savior's humili-
ation and death on the tree of shame; He has given Himself
to me to be my own, wholly and unreservedly my own—
my Maker, *my* Redeemer, and *my* unfailing Guide. And
that I may be assured and joyfully certain of my possession
God the Son, my Lord and Savior, gathered the Twelve
about Him on the eve of His passion and visibly gave Himself to them in the breaking of the bread and the passing
of the goblet. How simple the account, and how profound
and eternally meaningful the act! "And as they did eat,
Jesus took the bread, and blessed, and brake it, and gave
it to them and said, 'Take, eat: this is My body.' And He
took the cup, and when He had given thanks, He gave it
to them, and they all drank of it. And he said to them, 'This
is My blood of the new testament, which is shed for many.' "
Jesus gave Himself to the Twelve under the bread and the
wine; God gave Himself to man that man might be wholly
assured of the possession of God as his very own, of the
God of salvation. And when the divine Master said, "This
do," and thus indicated that this sacred rite was to be repeated by the believers, He made the assurance of this
possession mine when at the altar I partake of the consecrated bread and wine. I bend my knees, and my God un-

reservedly gives Himself to me, and with such assurance that my joy is full.

I am God's; God is mine; and more—God and I are one. God has completed the reconciliation with a visible sign, and in this reconciliation God and man have achieved an intimacy of union never enjoyed by Adam in the Garden of Eden. Now we are one in a manner far transcending my feeble comprehension; now we are forever one—Creator and creation, Redeemer and redeemed, Guide and wanderer. We are one on the way, and we shall be one at the goal. I am God's weakness, and He is my strength; for He dwells in me and I in Him. I am His yearning, and He is my fulfillment and my peace. He is the light that dwells in me; He is the love that moves in my heart, that finds utterance on my lips, that flows out of my hands in charitable ministrations. He is my perfect joy as of wings lifting me up in ever-widening circles of song.

A mortal was I born, but now by God's indwelling I am certified for eternity. I have within me life eternal; my life everlasting has surely begun even here on earth. Who would slay God? No more can I be slain, for by God's wondrous mercy and by His union with me He and I together shall face death down.

And now indeed do I have a foretaste of that heavenly life that is to be mine forever. Here am I still weakness, and God is strength, but daily does His strength flow into my weakness and firm it more and more. And daily is my vision of spiritual things strengthened by His light. Daily do I see and comprehend more clearly the beauty, the purity, the blissful selflessness, and the serene power of the life into which I shall grow. Oh, God dwelling in me has given me sweet and strange visions of the life His children are destined to live in that city seen of Patmian John. Rejoice, my soul, and be exceeding glad, for the days come, nor are they long in coming, when God will restore me and all believers, me and all who share in His holy body and blood, to that perfect state from which Adam in his blind willfulness fell what day he ate of the fruit forbidden. O joyous days, O blissful clime! Then and there in God's eyes shall our strong souls and minds and bodies employ their facilities in pristine strength and vie with one another in all that is pleasing to Him who on the sixth day and as the crown of his handiwork made man in His own image.

Before Thee, O merciful and gracious God, do I kneel me down with a heart running over with joy and praise. I praise Thee as Creator, I praise Thee as Redeemer, I praise Thee as Guide to the heavenly places. I praise Thee for the blessed plan of salvation; I praise Thee for Thy incarnation and for Thy death upon the lonely hill; I praise Thee for the call extended to me in Thy Holy Word and for Thy reception of me into Thy kingdom through the washing of regeneration; I praise Thee, oh, I praise Thee, for Thine invitation to this Holy Supper and for this divine union with me to the strengthening of my faith, my love, my zeal, and my joy, for Thine is the kingdom, and the power, and the glory forever and ever. Amen.

III

A DEDICATED DEPARTURE

THIS IS THE JOY

By Lewis Holm

↗ ↗ ↗

Read I John

"And we are writing this that our joy may be complete. This is the message we have heard from Him and proclaim to you, that God is light and in Him is no darkness at all. If we say we have fellowship with Him while we walk in darkness, we lie and do not live according to the truth; but if we walk in the light, as He is in the light, we have fellowship with one another, and the blood of Jesus His Son cleanses us from all sin. If we say we have no sin, we deceive ourselves, and the truth is not in us. If we confess our sins, He is faithful and just, and will forgive our sins and cleanse us from all unrighteousness. If we say we have not sinned, we make Him a liar, and His word is not in us,"
I John 1:4-10.

↗

The man who had called me to his bedside wanted to talk about what he had done. He thought it would help him to talk about it. It was my duty to listen, and I learned a great lesson. I learned that there is nothing sadder than a joyless Christian.

He was joyless because he was not sure that a sin he had committed more than twenty-five years before was forgiven. He was a slave to the haunting memory of what he had done in a moment of rage. His soul was bound with chains wrapped around it by his merciless conscience.

He had become during the twenty-five years since his lapse from his faith a model church member. He had grown in knowledge, he had become a good steward of the things which God had entrusted him, he had become a model husband and father. He attended church regularly and was a faithful communicant.

In twenty-five years he had received Holy Communion about 150 times. He had communed on the festival days such as Christmas, Easter, Pentecost, and Reformation, and on the ordinary days. He had communed in the morning and in the evening. He had taken Communion at district convention.

Yet he had not received assurance that his sin had been forgiven.

He spent hours in prayer, but he did not have assurance.

He spent evenings in witnessing, but he did not have assurance.

He had been baptized, instructed, confirmed, and married in the church. None of these things brought him assurance.

He was a baptized member, a confirmed member, a communicant member, a contributing member, a voting member of his congregation, but he wasn't sure God had forgiven him.

Because he was not sure that God had forgiven him he was not joyful.

A joyless Christian is a contradiction. How can a person be a Christian and not have joy? The angels brought the "glad tidings of great joy." The Savior said, "Ask, and ye shall receive, that your joy may be full." The apostle in chains said, "Rejoice! and again I say, Rejoice!"

The disciple John, in writing the words we are considering, says, "And these things write we unto you, that our joy may be full."

If the Christian has assurance of the forgiveness of his sins he is joyful no matter what he must suffer. The early Christians rejoiced that they were worthy to suffer for the name of their Lord Jesus. They flaunted their joy in the face of death, being assured that, whether they lived or died, they were the Lord's—knowing that to live is Christ and to die is gain.

If the Christian does not have assurance of the forgiveness of his sins he is not joyful, no matter what good things might happen to him. He may be active in church, he may become rich, he may have good health, a wonderful family, a fine name, and all kinds of blessings. Still he knows neither how to live nor how to die. He is a living tragedy, with eternal joy in his hand—and not closing his hand upon it.

God has more than that for His beloved people. His gospel is a gospel of joy. The Christian's joy is based on his assurance of forgiveness. We rejoice because we know that our sins are forgiven.

We know that our sins are forgiven for two reasons: first, God Himself assures us in His Word—second, God Himself gives us His own promise and pledge in the Lord's Supper.

We believe in the real presence of Christ in the Sacrament. We believe that we are receiving His true body and blood when we commune at His Table.

Now here is His promise: "The blood of Jesus Christ His Son cleanseth us from all sin."

Here it is again, in Romans 5:9: "Much more then, being now justified by His blood, we shall be saved from wrath through Him."

Again, in Hebrews 9:14: "How much more shall the blood of Christ, who through the eternal Spirit offered Himself without spot to God, purge your conscience from dead works to serve the living God?"

And in Revelation 1:5: "And from Jesus Christ, who is the faithful witness, and the firstbegotten of the dead, and the prince of the kings of the earth. Unto Him that loved us, and washed us from our sins in His own blood."

We receive His blood, and it is just that which cleanses us from all sin, saves us from wrath, purges our conscience, and justifies us.

We can be sure that our sins are forgiven in Holy Communion because we receive His blood, and it is His blood, and nothing else, that cleanses and washes and purges and saves.

The man who was confessing his sin had received Holy Communion 150 times and still didn't have assurance. Why not?

There are numerous reasons people don't have assurance even though they ought to have it. One reason is a lack of faith.

It is by faith that we must receive God's blessings in Communion. A few questions that determine the presence or absence of faith are these: Do you believe that Christ is truly present in His Supper? Do you believe that you actually receive His precious body and blood when you commune? Do you believe that He died on the cross in your place? Have you placed your sin upon Him and received Him as your personal Savior from sin and death? Do you believe that it is by His blood, which you receive in the Lord's Supper, that you are cleansed, washed, forgiven, justified, purged? Do you believe that God is both able and willing to remove your sin for the sake of His Son, Jesus

Christ, your Lord? Do you believe that God will do as He promises and cleanse you from all unrighteousness if you will simply confess your sins? (I John 1:9).

If we do not believe that Christ is truly present, and that He is gladly and completely forgiving our sins, we can't be joyful. We are truly of all men most miserable if we are still in our sins.

Another reason many Christians do not have assurance and joy is that they may not be genuinely repentant. John says: "If we say that we have fellowship with Him, and walk in darkness, we lie, and do not the truth."

No one can receive the Lord's blessings in Communion with tongue in cheek. The person who does not earnestly despise the sins which have separated him from God's closest fellowship simply cannot receive the joy. One must come with the earnest purpose, with the help of God, to avoid his sins in the future.

One who is genuinely repentant will not intend to go back to the old way as soon as the benediction has been pronounced. He is not at the Lord's Table to keep up the statistical record on his membership card or to keep the fine record of his congregation, district, or church. He is there to receive God's own assurance that his sins are forgiven. If he holds out on God, confessing some sins and hiding others, sorrowing over some and making mental reservations as to the others, he cannot receive joy because his conscience will not permit it. When we refuse to let God's Word enlighten our life and pierce through even to the shadows of our former questionable behavior we are at the same time refusing the joy that God wants us to have and the assurance that brings it.

The man who was bothered by his twenty-five-year-old sin appeared to be genuinely repentant and also to believe in Christ as his Redeemer and Savior. It was only after further questioning that he revealed another reason there are joyless Christians.

When he was asked, "Do you believe that God has forgiven you?" He answered, "Yes."

"Has the person or persons against whom you committed this sin forgiven you?"

"Yes." He seemed very sure about this. He had asked for forgiveness and had received it.

"If someone had done this very thing to you, would you have forgiven him?"

His answer was spontaneous. "Yes."

In spite of all these things bear in mind that the man had not had a day of peace in twenty-five years and was even now suffering for lack of peace and joy. It was only under further questioning that his real problem came to the surface.

"Have you forgiven yourself?"

The man was obviously puzzled when these words were addressed to him. He repeated them, "Have I forgiven myself?"

The question needed explanation. "You would gladly forgive another who might have committed the same sin against you—we have determined that. Now, aren't you willing to give yourself the same consideration? God has forgiven you, the other person has forgiven you, don't you owe it to yourself to forgive your own sin?"

He was thinking about it intently. "Do you not owe to yourself mercy as you owe it to others? You have a forgiving spirit—can you not apply it to yourself?"

He was still puzzled. He started to say something, and then his face changed, and the joy came through. "Yes!— I see it! Yes!"

For twenty-five years God and his fellow men had forgiven this man, but he had not forgiven himself. He had applied his spirit of generosity and forgiveness to everyone but himself. And he had not had joy for this reason.

The assurance of joy that this man received when he finally saw that he himself made his misery is important. One may have assurance without joy if he believes but still broods as this man did. When one is genuinely repentant, receives God's promised blessings by faith, and is willing to forgive himself he should have not only assurance but assurance and joy.

There's nothing sadder than a joyless Christian.

But there's nothing gladder than a Christian that is joyful.

And it seems that we can choose.

God of joy, when we behold what manner of love Thou hast bestowed upon us that we should be called Thy sons we tremble lest we despise any of Thy blessings. Grant unto us by Thy Spirit a full measure of assurance that our sins are forgiven by the blood of Jesus, our Savior, to the end that we may know the joy in this life and the next, of which the angels and the apostles spoke—through our union with Jesus Christ, Thy Son, our beloved Savior and Lord. Amen.

"THIS SALUTARY GIFT"

By Kurt C. Hartmann

✦ ✦ ✦

Read Romans, chapter 12

"Lord, now lettest Thou Thy servant depart in peace,
according to Thy word;
for mine eyes have seen Thy salvation
which Thou hast prepared in the presence of all peoples,
a light for revelation to the Gentiles,
and for glory to Thy people Israel," Luke 2:29-32 RSV

✦

I, a believer in Christ Jesus and a believer in His promises given in and through the words of institution, have participated in the celebration of the Lord's Supper. I have heard the word spoken by the minister, "Depart in peace." I walk away from the Lord's Table to my place in the house of God to thank Him for His "salutary gift."

I am still the same person. My body is the same. My mind and my soul are the same. I wear the same clothing. I am subject to the same calamities, heartaches, and joys, good days and evil days, to which I was subject before I communed with others at the Lord's Table. Other people are not visibly changed either. They are just as they were before. Neither they nor I have been immunized from sorrows and troubles and death. The assurance of better days also has not been given.

And yet . . . there *is* a difference. There *are* changes. There *should* be changes. There *will* be. It all depends on the *purpose* for which I participated in the celebration of the Lord's Supper. What was in my mind? my heart? my soul? when I walked to the Lord's Table? If I stood or knelt at the Lord's Table only to eat bread and to drink wine, truly, truly, I have my reward, and then some. That reward is destructive. Paul calls it "judgment" (I Corinthians 11:27, 29 RSV). If, on the other hand, I ate bread and drank wine, *believing* that at the same time Jesus was giving me His body and His blood; if, *in, with, under,* and *through* the bread and the wine I *saw* and *received* Christ's body and His blood; then I must depart with more than a "reward." Instead I leave the Lord's Table with a "salutary gift" from the Lord. "Salutary" means producing health; wholesome, beneficial; advantageous; promoting good.

For this "salutary gift" I am grateful. This gift has refreshed my spirit. To the degree that it refreshed my spirit it refreshed me totally: spirit, mind, and body; spiritually, mentally, and physically.

I, a sinner with a contrite heart and a broken spirit, have "seen." What have I seen? The Lord's *salvation.* It was wrapped up in the bread and the wine. I have seen His body and His blood, given and shed for me on Calvary's tree for the remission of sins. I have seen the forgiveness of sins. This was promised me *before* I came. But forgiveness was promised me also *as I received* the body and the blood of Christ.

If I was earnestly concerned, disturbed, wilted, bent, bowed down, and crushed by my sins as I approached the Lord's Table; if at the Lord's Table I permitted the word of the Lord, "For you for the remission of sins," to still and invigorate my disturbed and wilted soul, to straighten up my bent and bowed-down soul, and to give joy to my broken heart and contrite spirit, then I walk away with a newness of *inner life* which cannot be obtained elsewhere.

Christ has done something for me at His Supper Table. This Supper is different, poles apart from any other. It is a peculiar feast with heavenly blessings. Jesus has come to me under bread and wine. He has come to my spirit, to me as a believing person, and said, "This is *for you!*" Should all this be in vain? Should not everything that Jesus Christ puts into that *for you* result in many things *for Him?* Certainly. To that end I pray, if truly I pray.

Listen! "We give thanks to Thee, Almighty God, that Thou hast refreshed us with this Thy *salutary gift;* and we beseech Thee, of Thy mercy, to strengthen us through the same in faith toward Thee, and in fervent love toward one another;" etc. (See "The Thanksgiving" in the Communion Service.)

If I have been thinking, What a beautiful prayer the minister "says!" I have been missing something. That prayer is made by *me* as well as by *us* together with the minister. I must be praying, not only from and in the heart, I must be *heart*-praying as did Hannah of old. "My heart exults in the Lord," she said, "my strength is exalted in the Lord," I Samuel 2:1a RSV. The "we" must be turned into "I." "*I* give thanks . . . that Thou has refreshed *me* . . . and *I* beseech Thee . . . to strengthen *me* through the same."

What do I pray for together with others? The prayer is brief and to the point as well as pointed. Would that *we* and *I* considered this prayer more frequently and far more seriously than we do!

1.   First, I thank God. Giving of thanks and thankfulness are more than a matter of repeating words, only to be forgotten as soon as I leave the front door of God's house. Too often that is the case with me; out of mouth, out of

mind and heart. I thank God with my mouth, yes, but that gratitude must show itself in daily living, thanks-living, some call it. It is easy to "say" thanks. The true test is, Do I *live out* thanks?

For what am I grateful? The Lord has refreshed me with this "salutary gift," given me new strength, new courage, renewed my hopes, lifted up my soul, healed my broken heart, forgiven my sins once again. He has forgiven my sins countless times before. At His Table He came close to me, and it was as though He had stepped up to me *in person* and said to me, just me: "Given and shed *for you* for the forgiveness of sins. Here I give you My body, I give you My blood; that body which was nailed to the cross and that blood which flowed from that body—these I give *you* for the remission of sins." Everything that Christ did for me and gave to me is summed up in the two words, "salutary gift," and that is filling these two words to the brim and overflowing. Luther's statement, "Where there is forgiveness of sins, there is also life and salvation," may help to show how full these two words are.

2. After I have given thanks I, "Beseech Thee, of Thy mercy, to strengthen us through the same in faith toward Thee." It is the same request which the disciples made of their Lord, "Increase our faith." It is significant that this request came immediately after Jesus had spoken to them about forgiving one another. "Take heed to yourselves; if your brother sins, rebuke him, and if he repents, forgive him; and if he sins against you seven times in the day, and turns to you seven times, and says, 'I repent,' you must forgive him," Luke 17:3, 4 RSV. Thereupon came their request: "Increase our faith."

Does that say something to me who has just left the Lord's Table, has finished thanking the Lord for that "salutary gift" and now "beseech" (to entreat; implore; to beg; plead for) the Almighty God to strengthen me *in faith toward Him?* "Without faith it is impossible to please God," Hebrews 11:6. This faith which pleases God is a growing thing, not something which becomes smaller, or comes to a standstill to become stagnant as a pool of water. If faith is to continue to please God it must grow, it must increase, become stronger. It must become so strong that it forgives him who may sin against me not only once but seven times "in the day." The number seven stands for completeness or for times without enumeration so that the oftener he sins against me, the stronger and more willing I become to forgive him.

Too frequently it works the other way. A person is willing to forgive once, this once, just this once, but not oftener, never again. In that instance faith decreases, becomes weaker, eventually fades away into nothingness. "Strengthen us . . . me . . . in faith toward Thee." Increase my faith until it is like the faith of a grain of mustard seed and can say to "this sycamine tree, 'Be rooted up, and be planted in the sea,' and it would obey you." Jesus gave that as a reply to the apostles' request: "Increase our faith." Oh, for a faith that will grow, increase, become strong in and toward God! That kind of faith is ready to pray also:

3. "Strengthen us through the same . . . in fervent love toward one another." This "fervent love toward one another" is what the apostle sings about in the thirteenth chapter of his first letter to the Corinthians. "So faith, hope, love abide, these three; but the greatest of these is love." RSV. Why? Among other reasons because love is the proof that there is faith, that faith is real, alive, active, centered, anchored, and rooted in Christ and thus in God.

Jesus speaks at length about this love for one another. Hear Him: "A new commandment I give to you, that you love one another; even as I have loved you, that you also love one another. By this all men will know that you are My disciples, if you have love for one another," John 13: 34, 35 RSV. Does my prayer, "Strengthen me through the same in fervent love toward one another," begin to mean something? I pray, "Strengthen my faith, increase my faith." Must I not also pray, beseech, plead, "Increase my love toward my fellow believers"? Love increases in the measure that faith grows. If faith does not increase or decreases, love will follow the leader. If I love my fellow believer will I not forgive him, walk with him as the two disciples walked together to Emmaus when Jesus joined them, talk with him and encourage him to live with Jesus?

It is noteworthy that in the Service for the Communion of the Sick we find these same two points in the prayer of thanksgiving: "We beseech Thee, of Thy mercy, to strengthen *him* through the same, in faith toward Thee, in love toward all mankind." Even though the sick person be dying, it is of utmost importance, not only that his faith toward God be strengthened, but that his love be increased "toward all mankind."

At this point in my thinking I must return to a promise I made in the Confessional Service. In that service I promised, "Yes, it is my earnest purpose, henceforth, to be obedient to the Holy Spirit, to hate and forsake all manner of sin, to live as in God's presence, and to strive daily after holiness of heart and life." This is what the New Testament speaks of as walking in the Spirit. Paul writes about living in the Lord. Jesus speaks about abiding in Him.

This should come to light more and more in me from day to day, that I live as in God's presence, obey the Spirit of God by obeying the Word and the will of God. This is spoken of from two angles: 1. I must hate and forsake all manner of sin. 2. I must strive daily after holiness of heart and life. To illustrate: It is not sufficient for me to say, "I hate sin." I must also say, "I love God, I love my fellow believer, I love even my enemy," and prove all this by living as though God Himself were at my side.

In the book, *Flagellant on Horseback,* by Richard Ellsworth Day, it is said of David Brainerd by a Christian Indian, "Him not only TALK Jesus all the time, him LIVE Jesus all the time."*

In his letter to the Galatians the apostle Paul writes: "I have been crucified with Christ; it is no longer I who live, but Christ who lives in me; and the life I now live in the flesh I live by faith in the Son of God, who loved me and gave Himself for me," 2:20 RSV.

I have participated in the Lord's Supper in order that the transformation which Jesus accomplished in Paul might be accomplished in me. Repeatedly, therefore, I participate in the celebration of the Lord's Supper. My faith toward God cannot grow, my love toward all mankind cannot increase, unless I do participate in the celebration of my *Lord's Supper* often.

Lord, now let Thy servant depart in peace, to live a more thankful life. Let Thy "salutary gift" to me strengthen my faith toward Thee and increase my love toward all mankind. Amen.

---

* Richard Ellsworth Day, *Flagellant on Horseback,* p. 167. Used by permission of the publisher, The Judson Press.

ON MY WAY HOME FROM COMMUNION

By Edw. W. Schramm

↙ ↙ ↙

Read I Thessalonians 1

"We give thanks to God always for you all, making mention of you in our prayers; remembering without ceasing your work of faith, and labor of love, and patience of hope in our Lord Jesus Christ, in the sight of God and our Father. . . . For they themselves show of us what manner of entering in we had unto you, and how ye turned to God from idols to serve the living and true God; and to wait for His Son from heaven, whom He raised from the dead, even Jesus, which delivered us from the wrath to come,"

I Thessalonians 1:2, 3, 9, 10.

↙

I am on my way home from a Communion service at our church this Sunday morning. Fortunately, I live within walking distance of our church. That gives me a wonderful opportunity for meditation as I walk to and from church. I am not surprised that the Bible often refers to "walking with God." There is something about walking that suggests meditation . . . spiritual communion . . . fellowship with God. This noon I am meditating particularly upon the meaning of Holy Communion, and especially upon these questions: "What does God expect of me after I have been to Holy Communion? What effect should Holy Communion have upon my walking with God?"

Pondering these questions, I recall some words in the opening chapter of Paul's First Letter to the Thessalonians that seem to give a helpful answer. I remember that Paul, writing to the little congregation at Thessalonica, which he had established not many months before, told it that he was constantly remembering its "work of faith, and labor of love, and patience of hope in our Lord Jesus Christ." And I recall, too, that at the end of the chapter Paul explained what he meant by those three terms when he said that people everywhere were telling how the Thessalonian Christians had "turned to God from idols to serve a living and true God and to wait for His Son from heaven." Turning to God from idols . . . that, of course, is the work of faith. Serving the living and true God . . . that is quite evidently the labor of love. And there can be no doubt that waiting for His Son from heaven is the patience of hope.

Involuntarily I walk a little faster, for now I have some real light on my question, "What does God expect of me after I have been to Holy Communion?" I am sure that He expects of me *a closer walk with Him* because I have received the holy sacrament of the body and the blood of my Lord. And I am sure that the three great aspects of my walking with God are those three cardinal Christian experiences about which Paul wrote to the Thessalonians 1,900 years ago: The work of faith, the labor of love, and the patience of hope.

The work of faith . . . turning to God from idols. The Lord's Supper is without doubt designed to strengthen that gracious work of faith in my heart. I try to recall the circumstances under which Paul came to Thessalonica and the conditions that he found in that Macedonian seaport.

I remember, from Luke's account of the episode in the seventeenth chapter of The Acts, that Paul and his companions were treated shamefully at Thessalonica and could stay there only three weeks. But in that short time a little group of believers was gathered . . . some of them Jews, some of them Gentiles . . . from out of that wicked, unbelieving city.

Whether they held a Communion service during the short time that Paul was in Thessalonica the record does not say. Since Holy Communion was most highly regarded and frequently celebrated among the early Christians, it seems to me altogether likely that they did. And I can just imagine what a marvelous change came over those Christians at Thessalonica after the power of God had been brought to them through Word and Sacrament.

The Gentiles in that congregation had been worshiping idols—images and the pagan gods those images were supposed to represent. But the power of the gospel had turned them from the worship of dead idols to the worship of the living God and to a living faith in His Son Jesus Christ, the world's Redeemer and Lord.

Turning from idols to the living and true God! Say, that fits me, too! No, we have no images on our mantel at home before whom I fall down in worship. But there are idols in my heart . . . my own ego, my own pride, my self-will, my sinful devices and desires. There are idols, indeed, within me and about me that I am sorely tempted to worship, idols on which too often I set my mind and my affections. But I have just communed at the Table of my Lord! Through the bread and the wine the living, mighty Savior has come into my heart. And as I left the Communion altar, my pastor said to me, "The body of our Lord Jesus Christ and His precious blood strengthen and preserve you *in true faith* unto everlasting life." So God does expect me to walk more closely with Him because I have been at Communion this morning. And the first mark of that closer walk must be this that the work of faith is to be strengthened in me so that I turn from all idols to the living and true God.

It is really a splendid day for a walk. Above, the deep blue sky, broken here and there by a fleecy cloud. And around me the mingled shades of restful green. I pause to drink in the beauty of it all. And as I pause, the words of the Prayer of Thanksgiving at the end of the Communion service sound in my heart like the echoes of a strain in a majestic symphony: "We give thanks to Thee, almighty God . . . and we beseech Thee . . . to strengthen us . . . in faith toward Thee, *and in fervent love toward one another.*"

In faith toward Thee! That's first. And in fervent love toward one another! Yes, that's the second feature of a closer walk with God. And that is precisely what Paul told his Thessalonians: "Your work of faith and labor of love. You turned from idols to serve the living and true God."

Faith and love. God has joined them together, O my soul! For how can I turn from idol-worship and excessive love of self unless I turn to the worship and the love of Someone higher than I and greater than all idols? Faith worketh by love! Indeed, it does. And loving service of God is expressed by showing "fervent love toward one another," by serving the least of Christ's brethren.

So Holy Communion is designed to strengthen me in the labor of love . . . in Christian concern about others . . . in a kindly attitude toward all men, even my enemies . . . in interest in and support of such causes as Lutheran World Action and local welfare work.

Yes, it must be so! My conscience certainly tells me that I need divine strength and grace for such Christlike love, for I know from sad experience that, apart from the grace of God, I am, like Cain, inclined to deny that I am my brother's keeper; and, like the priest and the Levite, to pass my needy neighbor by. But this morning the living, loving Christ took hold of me in the Sacrament of His living presence . . . the same Christ who said on the night that He instituted the sacrament: "By this shall all men know that ye are My disciples, if ye have love one to another."

I have turned the corner and can see my home. Like a flash of inspiration the sight of my home brings vividly before me the final factor in a closer walk with God . . . the final thing which God must expect of me after I have communed. What can it be but the patience of hope . . . waiting . . . patiently waiting . . . for His Son from heaven . . . patiently waiting for the sight of my heavenly home . . . and living my days here and now in the light and in the power of that new and living hope which is mine through Jesus Christ, my Lord! And this morning . . . at the Table of the Lord . . . that glorious hope was strengthened as I communed with my fellow believers and with my Lord.

The patience of hope! I am comforted by the sure hope, the living hope that comes through Jesus Christ, the center of my faith and the inspiration of my love. And I remember that hope loomed large when my blessed Lord instituted the Holy Sacrament. "I say unto you, I will not drink henceforth of this fruit of the vine, *until that day when I drink it new with you in My Father's kingdom.*" So the Lord's Supper looks not only back upon what my Savior has done for me but also forward to the glorious consummation of all that is yet to be . . . forward to the eternal communion of all believers with their Lord and Master in the Father's kingdom.

The patience of hope! I am ashamed. For too often I have acted as though I had no hope; too often I have shown impatience instead of patience. But I have been to Communion today. And God expects of me that the patience of hope will mark my walk with Him because my life is hid with Him in Christ.

My walk is ended. I have reached my home. As I enter the house I sum up, for remembrance, the answer that I found on my way home to the important question, "What does God expect of me after I have been to Holy Communion?" My soul is satisfied that it is a good answer, a Scriptural answer: What does the Lord require of me but a closer walk with Him, marked by constant growth in the work of faith, the labor of love, and the patience of hope?

I give thanks to Thee, almighty God, that Thou hast refreshed me with this Thy salutary gift; and I beseech Thee, of Thy mercy, to strengthen me through the same in the work of faith, the labor of love, and the patience of hope; through Jesus Christ, Thy dear Son, my Lord, who liveth and reigneth with Thee and the Holy Ghost, ever one God, world without end. Amen.

PEACE IS DECLARED

By George H. Muedeking

✦ ✦ ✦

Read Romans 5:1-11

"Therefore being justified by faith, we have peace with God through our Lord Jesus Christ, by whom also we have access by faith into this grace wherein we stand," Romans 5:1, 2.

✦

Already Neville Chamberlain has taken his place as the most tragic figure of the twentieth century. The man came back from Munich to announce after his parley with Hitler that he had found "peace in our time." Within a few months of his statement World War II was flaming across the earth. This was not the first time humanity's hopes have been blasted; nor will it be the last. Our words declaring peace with each other cannot always be trusted.

Can they be trusted when they are spoken to us by God? "We have peace with God through our Lord Jesus Christ" —can these words be trusted? Of course they can, we say. Is it not God who speaks them? But then, why do we not believe Him? Why do we sometimes return from the Holy Supper without assurance that we are at peace with God?

Perhaps the problem does not rest with God at all, for it takes two parties to make peace. Perhaps the distrust of the peace treaty with God does not come because we cannot trust God's words, but because we cannot trust our own.

133

Peace can be maintained only when both parties to the treaty are trustworthy.

This is, no doubt, the heart of our difficulty. We recall that we have been to the Holy Communion before this day. We have remembered now what we did with that promise: "Poured out for you for the remission of sins": we have broken our half of the peace treaty. So war between God and ourselves broke out again. We are now uneasy and fearful that it may happen this time once more. We are afraid that we ourselves cannot be trusted. Therefore we cannot trust God either when He assures us that in Christ we are reconciled to Him. We cannot believe in our own reconciliation because we cannot trust ourselves to keep the peace treaty with God.

As we ponder our own untrustworthiness a little deeper we discover two reasons for it. First, we know that because of our spiritual weakness we shall sin again. We shall break our part of the treaty.

This in itself should not overwhelm us, however. For certainly, we are not the only ones who know our future. God also can see both what we are and what we shall do.

And this truth also we know full well. In fact, it was the searching understanding of the Lord, which He directed at our own heart, which first led us to Him. With the Samaritan woman we, too, can say concerning Jesus: "Come, see a man who told me all that I ever did; is not this the Christ?" Or with the Belgian student who told why his fellows were studying the Bible together during the war years we, too, can say: "Because this is the only Book that does not tell lies about man." Yes, it was this very searching understanding by our Lord which first led us to ask Him to take our weak and unsure hearts for Himself. We do know already that God declared peace with us in Christ, not because we are strong and unswerving saints, but because we are not strong. In his love He wanted to remake us into His own children in Christ.

So we understand that the forgiveness of God extends not only backward over the life we have followed thus far. It goes forward, too, taking into its cleansing power all that we shall ever do against His will. The forgiveness of God is like the air we breathe—here for our use at every moment we are on the earth. And this is also what the words tell us, "We have peace with God." For peace not only declares a conflict over, it declares the conflict is over for all the future. Peace always looks forward to the future of a standing reconciliation.

Then it cannot be merely that we think of our future transgressions when we doubt the certainty of God's forgiveness in this sacrament of forgiveness, His Holy Supper. The reason for the distrust of ourselves must lie more deeply hidden still. Perhaps it can be uncovered if we turn back to the betrayals of peace that we find among the nations.

Peace among nations is often destroyed because the treaty was signed with reservations. "We will keep our armies handy at the border in case the other side has not been honest," goes the thinking. But then a renewal of war is almost inevitable.

In the same manner we often view the peace treaty God has signed with us in the Sacrament. He has offered full forgiveness and His continuing presence and strength for every need.

But we are not sure. We do not know for certain that He means it. Perhaps in this or that area of our life it would be best to go on in the old way. To give that area of living over to God's control would be taking too much of a chance. So then we reason that it is best to keep these few areas of our living under our own control. For we do know already that we can get happiness out of them even if God were to fail us. At least that is what we believe.

These areas of living we do not surrender to God's peace offer are known by another name. They are our pet sins. We do not give them up—just in case God should fail to improve His strength and His care. The satisfaction we get from these pet sins are sure; but we are not so sure these satisfactions could be replaced by the hand of God with better satisfactions and surer happiness, were we to take His offer of love and leadership into every single part of our life without any reservations.

We are then really cheating the provisions of God's peace treaty with us. For it is made with the understanding that Christ should have the total right to our life. He would be our *Lord,* the Master of everything. The peace treaty with God in Christ stands as one Christian put it, "Christ wills to be Lord of all or not at all."

When we know deep within ourselves that we are thus cheating the provisions of God's peace treaty with us we, of course, distrust the future of the treaty. We come away from the Sacrament without peace with God because we do not expect that peace to hold. And we do not expect it to hold because we are unwilling to apply it in faith to every part of our life. We reserve for ourselves those areas of life where we are not able to believe in the completeness of God's blessing upon us.

But God knew about these reservations, too, when He offered His forgiveness. It was for them, too, that the precious blood was poured out. He invites us to try Him out even in these areas where we have been so unwilling to accept His control. When we do we shall know in our heart the peace of God that passes understanding. We shall know that we *have* peace with God through our Lord Jesus Christ.

Our blessed Lord, You won for us a total forgiveness when You died for us. You want us to believe this; You want us to accept the peace of God. Help us to give up each area of our life where we still question the blessing of Your control. Then we shall have Your peace as You want to give it to us. Amen.

"WITHOUT ME YE CAN DO NOTHING"

By G. E. Melchert

⟋ ⟋ ⟋

Read Galatians 5:16-25

"I am the vine, ye are the branches. He that abideth in Me, and I in him, the same bringeth forth much fruit; for without Me ye can do nothing.

"If a man abideth not in Me, he is cast forth as a branch, and is withered; and men gather them, and cast them into the fire, and they are burned.

"If ye abide in Me, and My words abide in you, ye shall ask what ye will, and it shall be done unto you.

"Herein is My Father glorified, that ye bear much fruit; so shall ye be My disciples.

"As the Father hath loved Me, so have I loved you: continue ye in My love.

"If ye keep My commandments, ye shall abide in My love; even as I have kept My Father's commandments, and abide in His love.

"These things have I spoken unto you, that My joy might remain in you, and that your joy might be full.

"This is My commandment, That ye love one another, as I have loved you. Greater love hath no man than this, that a man lay down his life for his friends.

"Ye are My friends, if ye do whatsoever I command you.

"Henceforth I call you not servants; for the servant knoweth not what his lord doeth: but I have called you friends; for all things that I have heard of My Father I have made known unto you.

"Ye have not chosen Me, but I have chosen you, and ordained you, that ye should go and bring forth fruit, and that your fruit should remain; that whatsoever ye shall ask of the Father in My name, He may give it to you.

"These things I command you, that ye love one another," John 15:5-17.

‍

In his matchless explanation of the First Article of the Apostolic Creed Luther says: "I believe that God has created me and all that exists . . . has given me food and raiment . . . daily provides abundantly for all the needs of my life." I believe this. I believe "His compassions fail not. They are new every morning: great is Thy faithfulness." I know that in times of great need He provided for His people in a miraculous way. In the Arabian wilderness He gave Israel manna from heaven. He commanded the ravens to bring bread and meat to Elijah while the prophet sat by the Brook Cherith; and when this same servant was in exile in the widow's house at Zarepath, "the barrel of meal did not waste, and the cruise of oil did not fail." And I read in my Bible that Jesus was moved with divine compassion and multiplied the bread and the fishes for the hungry multitude. I need food for my body. I need strength to do my daily task. I thank Him for His loving care.

I cannot, however, live by bread alone. I need food for my soul. I went to Holy Communion today. There was a struggle in my soul. With the assembled guests I sang:

> "Just as I am though tossed about
> With many a conflict, many a doubt,
> Fightings and fears within, without,
> O Lamb of God, I come, I come!"

I had experienced: "The flesh lusteth against the Spirit and the Spirit against the flesh: and these are contrary, the one to the other, so that ye cannot do the things that ye would." I looked upon myself, and the words of Paul became my confession: "I know that in me, that is in my flesh, dwelleth no good thing." I felt like the publican who "would not so much as lift up his eyes unto heaven." I felt like the father of the sick child who said to Jesus: "If Thou canst do anything, have compassion on us and help us." Then I remembered that my pastor had said many times: "When we come to the Lord's Table we do not come to a judgment throne but to a mercy seat." I knelt at the altar, and I heard those familiar words: "Eat . . . drink . . . this is given and shed for you for the remission of your sin." This was not merely bread and wine. My Lord was there. My Savior was there.

My heart beat lighter. My burden was lifted. The darkness vanished. He took off the spotted garment of my flesh. I heard Him say: "Though your sins be like crimson, they are as white as snow." I had not cleansed myself. He did this. All my efforts were in vain, for God had said: "Though thou wash thee with nitre and take thee much soap, yet thine iniquity is marked before Me," Jeremiah 2:22. Christ had washed me. I knew Him of whom John wrote: "He has washed us from our sins in His own blood." In my heart I felt the meaning of Paul's words: "You are washed; you are sanctified; you justified in the name of the Lord Jesus and by the Spirit of our God." Like the Ethiopian eunuch, I could go on my way rejoicing.

Christ had cleansed me; He had strengthened me. He is the vine; I am the branch. Without Him I can do nothing. He gives me strength for my soul. Tomorrow is an unknown land. No one has ever explored it. Satan may confront me with guile or with might. I am not afraid; Christ is with

me. Satan cannot conquer Christ. With the apostle Paul I
can say: "I know whom I have believed and am persuaded
that He is able to keep that which I have committed unto
Him." Tomorrow's burdens will be heavy, but I can cast
all my cares upon Him; He cares for me. The chaos and the
confusion of the world about me cannot frighten me. Why
should I be afraid? He said: "Be of good cheer; I have overcome the world." I am not alone. He does not merely stand
like a sentinel by my side; He lives within me. I can say:
"For me to live is Christ; to die is gain."

I know that His strength is sufficient unto me, "for I
am persuaded that neither death nor life, nor angels nor
principalities, nor powers nor things present nor things to
come, nor height nor depth nor any other creature shall be
able to separate me from the love of God which is in Christ
Jesus, my Lord." Without Him I can do nothing; but I know
that "He giveth power to the faint and to those who have
no might He increases strength. Even the youths shall
faint and be weary, and the young men shall utterly fall;
but they who wait upon the Lord shall renew their strength;
they shall mount up with wings as eagles; they shall run and
not be weary, and they shall walk and not faint." He said:
"Without Me ye can do nothing." One of His servants said:
"I can do all things through Christ who strengtheneth me."

He is the vine; I am the branch. The branch does not
bear fruit of itself. My strength to bring forth fruit comes
from Him. He speaks about fruit in His Word, and He
says: "Herein is My Father glorified, that ye bear much
fruit." These are not mechanical good works which I do
to be seen of men. I do not practice prayer, give alms to the
poor, or make pilgrimages to shrines in order to gain merit.
Those are self-chosen works, and they do not grow out of
faith. Christ strengthens me, and these are the fruits: "Love,

joy, peace, long-suffering, gentleness, goodness, faith." This is the life I live by faith in Christ who gave Himself for me. I live in fellowship with Him. I hear His voice and follow Him, and no man is able to pluck me out of His hand.

He strengthens me. He has given me more than He gave to those whose sightless eyes He opened; more than He gave to those lepers He cleansed; more than He gave to those who were infirm. He gives me strength. And I know I shall be numbered among those who shall sit at His table to eat of the heavenly manna and drink of the water of life.

He strengthens me. In His strength I live victoriously. I glory not in myself, I live to glorify Him. His love has conquered me, and with Paul I can say: "We are more than conquerors through Him who loved us." I grow in Him. He is the vine. The branch cannot bear fruit of itself. Without Him I can do nothing. He abides in me, and I in Him.

Precious Savior, Giver of life and strength, I thank Thee for Thy never-failing presence. Thou didst come to me to abide in me. Thou art the source of my strength and the rock of my help. In the midst of the changing scenes of life Thou art ever the same. Thou never failest. Thou didst give Thyself for me, and in the Sacrament Thou didst give Thyself to me. Thou art the Giver; I am the recipient of Thy gifts. I am weak; Thou art strong. I pray Thee, Lord and Savior, draw me into ever closer fellowship with Thee that by Thy strength I may grow to be like the tree that is planted by the water brooks that bringeth forth its fruit in its season. From day to day let me live my life unto Thee to glorify Thee. I know that Thou art able to do exceeding abundantly above all that I ask or think; but give me strength sufficient unto each day and at length, when my earthly pilgrimage is done, receive me into Thy presence with exceeding joy. I ask this in Thy name. Amen.

TILL HE COME

By L. E. Eifert

✐ ✐ ✐

Read II Corinthians 5:17-21

"For as often as ye eat this bread and drink this cup ye do show the Lord's death till He come," I Corinthians 11:26.

✐

The words "till He come" project our thoughts into the future. Jesus is coming again. The Lord clearly taught that "the Son of man shall come in His glory, and all the holy angels with Him," Matthew 25:31. With divine sanction Jesus stated that the "Father hath given Him authority to execute judgment also, because He is the Son of man," John 5:27. The holy apostles gave repeated expression to their belief in the doctrine of the second coming of Christ. They remembered clearly the words of the angels who at the Lord's ascension into heaven said, "This same Jesus, which is taken up from you into heaven, shall so come in like manner as ye have seen Him go into heaven," Acts 1:11. On such and many other unmistakable statements of the Holy Bible the church bases its conviction, so confidently expressed in the Nicene Creed, "And He shall come again with glory, to judge both the quick and the dead, whose kingdom shall have no end."

In the words of our text St. Paul associates the second coming of Christ with the Sacrament of Holy Communion. Having reminded the Corinthian Christians in the two preceding verses of the solemn institution of the Lord's Supper, he tells them that, as often as they eat this bread and drink this cup, they "do show the Lord's death *till He come.*" Until that awesome moment when all the nations of the earth shall be gathered before the Son of man for judgment; until that great and glorious day when the King of kings and Lord of lords will return to gather His own into His heavenly kingdom; until that day dawns, the day of fulfilment for the believers and the day of divine retribution for the unbelievers, we are to show the Lord's death in the Sacrament of the Altar.

On the sojourn through this brief span of life to our eternal home in heaven Holy Communion ought to mean much to us. For the body and the blood of Christ, given us in the Sacrament, are the pledge of our heavenly citizenship, and they strengthen and sustain us on the journey toward the complete enjoyment of this citizenship.

I

As we partake of Holy Communion, says St. Paul, we "show the Lord's death," we proclaim to all men that Christ died. It is a joyful proclamation. To announce the death of a dear friend or of a member of the family may be a sad assignment. But to let it be known that Christ died, ah, that we can do with deep satisfaction. The Lord's death was not a tragedy. It took place by the determinate counsel and foreknowledge of God. God's eternal love looked down upon a world lost in sin, upon a human family that had sinned and gone astray and was headed for eternal doom and destruction. In His eternal love God determined to save His people from their sins, to bring them back to the heavenly household from which they had strayed. God's eternal love brought a tremendous sacrifice: His only-begotten Son became a member of His people and died for them upon the accursed tree of the cross. By this death atonement was made for the sins of mankind. "We are reconciled to God by the death of His Son," Romans 5:10. "He who knew no sin was made sin for us, that we might be made the righteousness of God in Him," II Corinthians 5:21.

And when I go to the Lord's Supper I am letting it be known that I believe that Christ died for me. I hear again those words which the Lord spoke on the night in which He was betrayed: "This is My body which is given for you. This cup is the new testament in My blood which is shed for you." These words, "for you," require of me to confess that I am a sinner; they require of me to realize what a grievous thing every one of my sins is, so grievous that my Lord, the Son of God, had to shed His blood for me. But above all, the words "for you" require of me to believe that in Christ's holy, precious blood I am cleansed from all guilt and iniquity, that God again looks upon me as His own dear child, a member of His household, an heir of heaven. And to strengthen me in that blessed conviction I receive, under the bread and the wine, the true body and blood of the Lord, the body that was nailed to the cross, the blood that was shed when my dear Savior gave Himself for me.

What a marvellous pledge of our heavenly citizenship! Without it we look into the future with fear and uncertainty; without it the words, "till He come," hold for us no comfort, no joyful anticipation, but only a terrible waiting for the Master's return and the inevitable judgment. God had something better in mind for us when He sacrificed His Son on Calvary's cross. "I am come," said Jesus, "that they might have life, and that they might have it more abundantly," John 10:10. Such an abundant life presupposes peace of mind, peace of conscience, peace with God. We must have the assurance that our sins are pardoned and forgiven. To this end God has given us the gospel of salvation through Jesus Christ, which is "the power of God unto salvation to everyone that believeth," Romans 1:16. And the visible pledge of salvation, one that we can see and feel, we have here in the Holy Supper, where Jesus Himself comes to us in the lowly elements of bread and wine in order to dwell in our heart, to assure us of our home in heaven, "till He come," until the day of His visible return when He will gather His own to live and to reign with Him eternally.

II

When Jesus began His public ministry and called His first disciples, one of them, Nathanael, expressed great amazement that the Lord should know so much about him. Jesus told him: "Thou shalt see greater things than these. . . . Verily, verily, I say unto you, hereafter ye shall see the heavens open, and the angels of God ascending and descending upon the Son of man," John 1:50, 51. Surely, we recognize Holy Communion as one of these "greater things." The presence of Christ in the Sacrament affords us a glimpse into the open heaven. The blessed Communion with our Savior is already a foretaste of our heavenly home. But until we attain full citizenship in heaven you and I are still strangers and pilgrims on this earth. We live in a world that is not mindful of its eternal destiny. Men and women have set their heart on earthly treasures, on wealth, power, and pleasure. They think only of their earthly needs. They ask, "What shall we eat, what shall we drink, wherewithal shall we be clothed?" Mistakenly they think that their future is assured by their bank accounts, life insurance, health and accident insurance, or social standing.

We must not permit ourselves to be carried away by this stream of worldliness; we must not let our vision of "till He come" be overshadowed by the ambitions that the world has set for itself. We must give heed as the Sacrament of the Altar loudly proclaims the Lord's death. We sometimes want to go along with the world on its path of godlessness. We see so much dishonesty, so much uncleanness, so much indulgence in sinful pleasures, so much greed and lust for power; we tell ourselves, "Everybody is doing it, why shouldn't I?" But the Sacrament proclaims the death of our Lord, and the death of our Lord took place to atone for just those sins in our life that we try so hard to excuse and cover up. The death of the Lord is all that we need to convince ourselves that the way of the righteous and the way of the ungodly lead in opposite directions. Dear friend and fellow pilgrim, the Sacrament of the Altar affords you a glimpse of the open heaven; don't let the earth's glitter and tinsel spoil that view of your future home; don't let the noise and the clatter of this world drown out the song of the angels.

St. Peter tells his hearers, "Dearly beloved, I beseech you as strangers and pilgrims, abstain from fleshly lusts which war against the soul," I Peter 2:11. That's direct language. Of His children who are on their journey to heaven God expects that they keep their soul clean, pure, unsullied. Nothing that is sinful, unclean, unholy will be permitted to pass through the portals of eternal life. It is expected of Christians that they grow in godliness and good works. A Christianity that is satisfied to rest on its laurels is a dead religion. Perhaps you are harboring a hatred in your heart, a grudge against one of your fellow pilgrims. You know that is wrong, but you refuse to cast that hatred out. You tell yourself that you have lived with it all this time, a little longer will do no harm. That is not Christian thinking. As soon as we begin to feel satisfied with ourselves as we are, especially if we let any form or manifestation of sin live in our heart and do not make an honest effort to cast it out, we are no longer proclaiming the Lord's death. The Lord's death on the cross was intended to bring about a change in us; the Lord's death is the basis for a complete regeneration. St. Paul makes that plain. "If any man be in Christ, he is a new creature; old things are passed away; behold, all things are become new," II Corinthians 5:17.

Since Holy Communion is a proclaiming of the Lord's death and the expression of our faith in the full atonement that was made for our transgressions, it is to be expected that our continued attendance at the Lord's Table will bring about a change in our thinking and our actions, when such a change is necessary. We ought to be better Christians because we have the opportunity of going frequently to Holy Communion. Even as earthly food strengthens our body and helps in its growth and its development, so in a spiritual manner ought the body and the blood of Christ, which become a part of our being through the eating and the drinking in the Sacrament, bring about growth in faith, in love, in godliness, in good works.

You may often tell yourself, of course, that you have noticed no appreciable change in yourself after going to Holy Communion. You may have had good intentions to give up this sin or that, but you have weakened again and given in. But remember, the old evil foe, Satan, will not easily be downed; the battles we wage against the devil are constant ones. And that is all the more reason that we must put on the gospel armor, and that we must often strengthen ourselves with the heavenly food that is given us in the Sacrament of the Altar. Remember also that "God is faithful, who will not suffer you to be tempted above that ye are able; but will with the temptation also make a way to escape, that ye may be able to bear it," II Corinthians 10:13.

Thus God in His mercy has given us strength and sustenance on our pilgrimage to heaven. In His great love He has prepared for us a home in heaven; Christ's death assures us of that. And that we may not wander on strange paths nor grow weary of the way of righteousness God has seen to it that the death of His Son should for all times be proclaimed. May our faith and our life be a constant witness to God's grace as we, eating the bread and drinking the cup in the Sacrament, show the Lord's death till He come.

Strengthen and sustain us, we pray Thee, gracious God, as we pass the days of journeying to our heavenly home with Thee. Impress on us the image of Thy Son, Jesus, who gave His body and shed His blood for our sins. Keep us day by day in the way of faith and righteousness. As we eat the bread and drink the cup in the Sacrament, let Jesus rule our heart and our life. Direct all our thoughts heavenward and keep us in body and in soul till He come. Through Jesus Christ, our Lord. Amen.

THIS IS PEACE!

By Herman Mees Meyer

⚹ ⚹ ⚹

Read Psalm 86

"Lord, now lettest Thou Thy servant depart in peace, according to Thy word: For mine eyes have seen Thy salvation," Luke 2:29, 30.

⚹

It happened a long time ago. And yet I remember almost every detail. It happens, I suppose, in the ministry of every pastor. There are incidents we do not easily forget. I had gone to the church office early. There was an accumulation of important work to be done before the phone would ring, and the activity of an unusually busy day would begin. How stimulatingly quiet it can be right after seven o'clock on a May morning! And then—I could hardly believe my ears— the phone was ringing. Who in the world would call a church at that time of the day! "Pastor, is that you? Oh, I'm so glad. I just knew you would answer. I just knew it!" Thus the distressed female voice: "I've hardly had any sleep all night. And I can't put it off any longer. I just must talk to you. Could it be sometime today, the sooner the better?" I looked at my pretty well filled schedule and replied on the impulse of the moment: "It's early. But can you come right now?" "Oh, pastor, I was hoping you would say that. The lady next door I know will take care of my baby, and I should be there in twenty minutes."

Less than twenty minutes later in the bright stillness of that spring morning she was telling me the story back of the sleepless night, back of many such nights. Hers was a happy marriage of some two years. She had a fine husband and a sweet little daughter. But that dark cloud, that cloud that so frequently closed in on her soul, just wouldn't leave permanently. It always came back, chiefly at night. Before her marriage she had been private secretary to a man whose home life was not happy. His difficulties and his disappointments he had finally confided in her, and she had been sympathetic in her understanding. Against her better judgment she yielded to his pleading and accepted a dinner invitation. It became a weekly habit and finally led to an affair. Though all that had been ended three years before, the weight of its remembrance grew heavier and heavier. That gnawing sense of guilt. That fear. That feeling of smothering. Her husband knew nothing of it. She had been afraid to tell him. He was so kind and good and true. But she could stand it no longer. Something had to be done. But what?

That she was deeply penitent could not be doubted. Had she made confession to God? Many times. Had she asked God for forgiveness? Yes, night and day. Had she communed with her Lord in the Sacrament? Yes, just two Sundays ago. Had she not heard the announcement in the confessional service that her sins were forgiven? Yes. Had she not taken the cup and heard the blessed words: "Take and drink, this is the blood of the New Testament, shed for thy sins"? Had not the blood of Christ made her clean of all sins, even that sin which still lay so heavy on her heart? She didn't know. That was the trouble. She didn't know. She didn't think so.

It was still early when she left. And the phone had not rung again. In her presence I had asked God to direct me. Both of us knew that He did. She and I had gone into the chancel. She had knelt before the altar and literally told God everything. She blurted it out like the hurt but confiding child she was—her sins, her doubts, her fears, her heartaches. She had received absolution. She had had private Communion. When she spoke the words of the *Nunc Dimittis,* "Lord, now lettest Thou Thy servant depart in peace, according to Thy word; for mine eyes have seen Thy salvation," she had really found peace. There was no doubt of that. It was in the expression on her face. It was in the joy that lighted her eyes. It was in the spring of her step as she walked out of her church and simply said: "This is peace! Thank God."

Peace where there had been no peace. What had happened? What had at long last brought release from the dull, heavy terror of a troubled conscience? How had she found this peace? I think she must have recognized the road to her peace in the ancient words which came from her lips almost as a sigh as she said: "Thy servant depart in peace *according to Thy word;* for mine eyes *have seen Thy salvation.*"

Hers was peace according to the Word of God, for it was there that she had found it. On the corner of my desk there lay a somewhat soiled and faded little book. As I reached for it I saw that she recognized it. Twelve years before she had used one like it in her senior confirmation class. Yes, she still had her catechism somewhere, she told me, but somehow had never thought of using it in her trouble. It wasn't difficult to find the Scripture passages which applied to her situation in that little book. There they were under the lesson on the Conclusion to the Ten

Commandments, that on the Forgiveness of Sins in the Third Article of the Creed and the Explanation of the Fifth Petition of the Lord's Prayer. We read them over. She remembered some of them. They had been part of her memory work in preparation for her confirmation.

While she was literally staring at all those passages that spoke of sin and seeing them as she admitted in a new light, I had reached for another book, a volume of sermons preached years before by a pulpit hero of my college days, the late Charles E. Jefferson of New York City. "Listen to these words and I think you will make a discovery about those passages," I suggested. Thereupon I had read a few sentences that I had long ago underscored: "When the Bible touches sin it grasps it with the rough hand of a man in earnest. It acknowledges the presence of it, confesses the reality of it, it emphasizes the malignity and the awful danger of it, and stirs up in the heart a passionate desire to get rid of it. That fact is the only thing essential . . . . It is enough to know that sin is a burden to the heart of God, and that God has provided a way for our deliverance."[1] "Now examine every one of those passages," I continued, "and you cannot help but see what a burden sin, all sin, your sin is to the heart of God, for it seems that God cannot talk about sin without also talking about forgiveness and cleansing and the cross. Listen to John, the close friend of Jesus: 'If we say that we have no sin, we deceive ourselves. If we confess our sins, He is faithful and just to forgive us our sins and to cleanse us from all unrighteousness,' I John 1:8, 9. And the apostle Paul: 'The wages of sin is death, but the gift of God is eternal life through Jesus Christ our Lord,' Romans 6:23. Who can read such state-

---

1. Charles E. Jefferson, *Things Fundamental,* pp. 228, 229. Used by permission of the publisher, Thomas Y. Crowell Company.

ments and not know and feel in his heart that God desperately *wants* to forgive sins?"

We kept on reading, she and I, in that little catechism, "All we like sheep have gone astray, and the Lord hath laid on Him the iniquity of us all," Isaiah 53:6. We looked at II Corinthians 5:21 and found that the new translation of the New Testament Epistles called *Letters to Young Churches* made it so much clearer: "For God caused Christ, Who Himself knew nothing of sin, actually to *be* sin for our sakes, so that in Christ we might be made good with the goodness of God."[2] "Don't you see," I asked, "that God not only wants to forgive sins, but He went the whole way to make forgiveness possible? It cost Him the highest price ever paid, the life of His own Son, all in order that what God would do, He *could* do." "Look at that cross on my desk," I said. "Look hard at it. Don't you see now what it really means, namely, that God in Christ can and will forgive *every* sin when the penitent sinner really wants that forgiveness?" "Yes, pastor, I see that. But does it include also this feeling of guilt, all this pressure on my conscience that chokes me whenever I look at my precious, innocent baby lying asleep in her little bed and think of her fine, decent father? You know, pastor, there are times that I blame myself as much as I blame that woman. Excuse me, I mean my former employer's wife. If she only would have been a better wife, I would never have gotten into this predicament. How can God forgive me when I can't forgive myself, when I can't forgive her?"

There was a long silence after that outburst. And then came an admission: "You know, pastor, I've never said that to anyone before, I mean that 'I can't forgive her.' I've

---

2. Phillips, *Letters To Young Churches,* p. 78, (1951). Used by permission of the publisher, The Macmillan Company.

never even said that to God." Thoughtfully she began leafing through the catechism on my desk as if looking for something long lost. It took some time before she traced her finger down a little past the middle of a page and exclaimed: "There it is. I knew I had memorized those words, 'If ye forgive not men their trespasses, neither will your Father forgive your trespasses,' Matthew 6:15. I haven't done that, pastor. That woman haunts me. How can I forgive her? It was really she who spoiled my life. Yet I want to forgive. I know I should. Why don't I?"

While she had been leafing through the catechism, I had been doing the same with my copy of *Letters to Young Churches*. I, too, had traced my finger down a page in Paul's Letter to the Romans: "My own behavior baffles me. For I find myself not doing what I really want to do, but doing what I really loathe . . . . I often find that I have the will to do good, but not the power . . . . It is an agonizing situation, and who on earth can set me free from the clutches of my own sinful nature?" She interrupted. "Why, that's a picture of me, pastor. And that question Paul asks, that's been my question for months." "But let me finish reading," I asked and then read very slowly Paul's answer to his own question. She heard the words which seemed to remove the last road block to peace: "I thank God there is a way out through Jesus Christ our Lord."[3]

She saw it all now. It was God's Word which came to her in the fullness of its truth and its blessing that had taken her step by step along the road to peace. She had not forgiven another. It was so hard. Yet now it was clear, it could be done through Christ, through the indwelling Christ. She remembered Paul's witness to that "I can do all things through Christ which strengtheneth me," Philippians 4:13.

3. *Ibid.*, pp. 16, 17.

The words of the institution of the Lord's Supper seemed to become alive for her, "This is My body . . . . take drink, this is My blood." "What can that mean," she queried, "but that Christ *can* actually live in me?"

Again her memory became vocal, and she was repeating words she thought she had forgotten: "Given and shed for you for the remission of sins. For beside the bodily eating and drinking these words are the chief thing in the Sacrament." At that point I joined her in Luther's explanation of how the eating and the drinking of the bread and the wine in the Sacrament could confer such great benefits, and together we said, "And he who believes them has what they say and declare, namely, the remission of sins." Nothing was said after that until she said it. "I do believe those words. I really do." And she did. The muscles of her face, the tendons in her neck, her position on her chair, all gave evidence that the weight had been lifted, and the feeling of guilt had gone. She had found Christ's peace.

All those three years she had quite neglected God's Word. Furthermore, she had looked at her problem horizontally. Her eyes had been fixed on man's way of thinking and doing. She had found it too difficult for her to forgive. She couldn't understand then how God could forgive. And to forget—well, that was just impossible. Then how could God forget? And if He didn't forget, even if He had forgiven, the thing was still there, still being held against her, and that meant guilt. She had forgotten that Christ was lifted up on a cross so that God could forgive and forget. She had forgotten that the eyes of a sinful man could not discover the truth when they just looked across at other sinful men, but only when they looked up to the God-man on that cross, there to behold that God's ways are higher than man's ways. "For mine eyes have seen Thy salvation."

These were not only aged Simeon's words, but her words that morning at the Communion rail. Do you see now why she walked out of her church, saying simply: "This is peace! Thank God."

Such was a true experience in one life. It can be a true experience in many lives. Perhaps in yours.

Oh, Spirit of the living God, let me behold day by day wondrous things in Thy Word, the things that meet my daily difficulties and make for my peace. Accept my thankfulness for the blessed sacrament of reconciliation where the Word is made visible and tastable and touchable to me, the Word that brings complete pardon and the peace that passes understanding. Hear my prayer, Holy Spirit, in the name of Jesus Christ who through the Word and the Sacrament actually comes into my life. Amen.

OUR HEARTS REJOICE

By John E. Meyer

✦ ✦ ✦

Read Romans 8:26-39

"And Jesus came and spake unto them, saying, 'All power is given unto Me in heaven and in earth . . . . and lo, I am with you always, even unto the end of the world,' "

Matthew 28:19, 20b.

✦

A famous surgeon once performed an extremely dangerous operation while several distinguished doctors watched. When the operation was successfully completed, someone asked him how he could work so calmly with critical eyes watching his every move. "When I operate," replied the surgeon, "there are just three present: the patient, myself, and God." And God! Such an unwavering assurance of God's presence in our life is the highest point of Christian living. Our text brings us face-to-face with the reality of God's powerful presence in our life. He is present with His power because He gave us a will to believe and a command to obey; indeed, He gave us a life to live in a manner that will increase His glory and extend His kingdom.

And His presence in our life with power must be a reality. We must believe it, we must be conscious of it, we must be assured of it. Such an assurance can remake our life from top to bottom. Our spiritual life may seem weak; yet by knowing the presence of His power it can become strong and courageous. Life may seem to be without purpose, we may be deep in frustration, doubt, fear, and anxiety; yet by the awareness of His presence we can be cleansed and renewed, our life can have meaning again, and we can rejoice.

Time and time again this happened to men in the Bible. Men like Moses, Isaiah, Ezekiel, and Paul literally became new men, with new courage, new zeal for serving God, when they realized that God was with them with His power and His strength. Someone has said a religious man is one who has a ruling sense of God's presence. And it's true. Nothing can equip a life with courage, peace of mind, and hope like looking straight into the face of God and believing Him when He says, "I am with you always." Nothing can steady our feet more surely than to experience the all-conquering power of God in our life and believe that "we are more than conquerors through Him that loved us," Romans 8:37.

We speak of the "real presence" of Christ in the Sacrament of Holy Communion. Is it true? He said it, and we believe it: "This is My body, this is My blood, given for you." Surely, the most vital element in the Sacrament is that we believe in His presence. Without His presence it can hardly be a genuine spiritual strengthening. If it is just a memorial feast, then the burden of making Communion mean something real in our life lies with us, in all our weakness and sinfulness, and not with God. If there are power and strength available in Holy Communion, they must come from God, and our heart rejoices when we realize anew that Christ is indeed present—His body and His blood—in the Sacrament of Holy Communion.

Believing that He is present, I want to suggest three ways in which the Lord's Supper can mean spiritual strengthening for our life.

The first is this: *in Holy Communion we discover God's friendliness.* We may know that God is holy, yet feel that we dare not approach Him. We may know that He is wise, yet fear to come into His presence. We may know that He is mighty, yet feel like dust and ashes as we draw near to Him. But if we can behold His love, if we can know Him as a friend, whose greatest concern is our happiness, then our life may be enriched by His presence, and we may rejoice. We do behold His love in Holy Communion as nowhere else. For here is Christ, the only-begotten Son, given because God loved the world so completely that He was willing to sacrifice the very best He had to give.

A girl ran away from home one day. Her mother found her several days later, miserable, lonely, and destitute. When they got back home, the girl refused to go into the house. "I can't go in, I have done wrong, I can't face father," she said. The mother assured her that her father was longing for her to come home, that he was hungering to see her again. While the girl was hesitating, the father came out of the house and with his strong arms warmly embraced his daughter. Suddenly all of the girl's fears were gone, and she was happy to be home.

Such is the exciting message of Holy Communion. The friendliness and the love of God are here revealed in all of their glory; not because we come claiming any right to be loved, but because He comes to us, loving us while we are yet sinners. In Holy Communion we may feel at home, we need never feel that we are strangers encountering a God who can't be known. Indeed, the presence of Christ in Holy Communion means that God is our friend, that He is our companion, walking with us on every road, no matter where it leads.

Experiencing then the friendship of God, we are strengthened, our life is renewed, and our heart rejoices.

Now second: *in Holy Communion we realize a new fellowship with one another.* In the early Christian Church Christ's followers were identified by their love for one another. Together they had seen the living Christ, witnessed His crucifixion, and beheld Him in His resurrected glory. As they became conscious of His presence in their life they were welded into a fellowship that knew no bounds.

We, too, need desperately to discover this fellowship with one another in Christ Jesus. And where else can this oneness be more surely experienced than in Holy Communion, where we join together in a common confession of our sins, hear together the assurance of forgiveness, and together partake of His precious body and blood? If we are missing this stirring fellowship with one another in Christ we are missing one of the really towering blessings of Christian life.

"A new commandment I give unto you, that you love one another; even as I have loved you, that you also love one another," John 13:34. As we realize this oneness that exists between those who are in Christ, our life is strengthened. No longer do we stand alone—one small life lost in the mass of humanity. We are rather a part of a great fellowship with men and women who, like ourselves, have surrendered their life to the Savior. Men and women with the same hope, the same faith, and the same love. Men and women who have dedicated their life to One, and in Him they live and move and have their being.

As we realize this fellowship in Holy Communion; as we join our lives to behold the glory of God in Christ Jesus— His body and His blood—we are strengthened, our lives are renewed, and our hearts rejoice.

In Holy Communion our life is strengthened because we discover God's friendship, because we realize a common fellowship, and this is third: *because we experience Christ's forgiveness.*

If Holy Communion doesn't mean that our life is really strengthened through complete and total forgiveness, then it means nothing. If it doesn't assure us of eternal life, then it's foolish to be so concerned about it. But it does. Listen to the words of Christ: "He who eats My flesh and drinks My blood has eternal life, and I will raise him up at the last day," John 6:54. There are no "ifs" about His words. Those who depend upon His body and His blood for forgiveness and eternal life shall have them. Can anyone remain spiritually downcast, knowing that eternal life is his beyond a shadow of doubt? Where are our fears, our worries, our anxieties when we hear this assurance of complete forgiveness? Where is our feeling of hopelessness and despair when we have this positive assurance of eternal life? Gone! Lost forever in the everlasting love, grace, and mercy of God.

We are cleansed, assured, and therefore strengthened when we bring every sin before His throne of mercy. And that means *every* sin. Nothing dare be held back, no sin allowed to remain unconfessed. Every sin of faithlessness, every act of selfishness, intolerance, or lust, every sacrifice we have been unwilling to make for His sake, every unclean word or thought, every bit of self-centeredness—every one must be here confessed and thrown down at His feet that He might burn them away by the scalding fire of forgiveness.

Rejoice our hearts! Our hearts rejoice! Measure the value of forgiveness if you can. Measure it in terms of peace of mind, peace of soul, sense of assurance, sense of being right with the Creator, life's purpose. Measure it in terms of faith and trust and confidence. Yes, "we are more than conquerors through Him who loved us"; through Him who has all power; through Him who is with us always.

Does Holy Communion really renew and strengthen our life? Does anything else? Can Holy Communion cause our heart to rejoice? Indeed! "And your hearts will rejoice, and no one will take your joy from you . . . ask, and you will receive, that your joy may be full," John 16:22b, 24b.

Holy Communion means this: we discover God's friendship, we realize our common fellowship, and we experience Christ's forgiveness, and our heart rejoices.

Our God and Father: lift up our heart. Teach us to know the joy of Thy salvation through the body and the blood of our beloved Savior. By Thy grace restore in our heart the true meaning of Holy Communion so that we might feel the power for our life and the joy for our heart which Thou hast prepared for us. We rejoice and give thanks for His death and His suffering which have made it possible for us to be called the sons of God. We pray in our Savior's name. Amen.

A DEDICATED DEPARTURE

By George W. Scheid

✔ ✔ ✔

Read Galatians 5:16-28

"Lord, now lettest Thou Thy servant depart in peace, according to Thy word; for mine eyes have seen Thy salvation, which Thou hast prepared before the face of all people," Luke 2:28-32.

✔

I, who call myself a Christian and yet know myself as a poor sinner, have knelt in the confession of my sins; I have declared my faith in the forgiveness which my Savior promises to repentant sinners; I have promised in the power of the Holy Spirit to amend my sinful life. I have heard the declaration of God's grace and the forgiveness of my sins in the name of the Lord Jesus Christ pronounced by my pastor. I have stood at the altar and there received the bread of life and the wine of salvation. The servant of the Lord has sent me away with a prayer and a blessing of peace.

Now what? Is this spiritual transaction between me and my Lord all ended with a few closing responses of thanksgiving and praise? What has happened to me in the Holy Communion? What am I taking with me from that holy altar? What will God and man see in my life as a result of this day's holy experience?

What did I really receive in the Communion? The forgiveness of my sins? Yes, but Jesus had already given me

His promise and the actual declaration of forgiveness in the confessional service before the Communion. However, then it was given to me with the whole congregation of believers and confessors. And that was a truly valid promise and declaration.

But here in the Holy Supper that forgiveness was personalized and individualized for me in a very special manner by my Lord Himself. I heard His own words which are as effective today and forever as they were on the day He first spoke them. And they were here spoken to me, spoken to me individually and personally. Like a mother whose little flock of children has been naughty and has expressed sorrow and been forgiven by her. But one sensitive little fellow comes back alone and wants to be sure that he was really included, and she draws him to her heart and with word and caress and kiss assures him that he was and is really forgiven.

But Jesus here goes even farther. He pledges His inviolable word to me personally with a visible seal and surety and guaranty, the very body and blood in which and through which He wrought that forgiveness and life and salvation for me.

The president stamps the seal of the great government of the United States upon a document to certify his signature and his authority and to pledge and to guarantee the protection and the power of the government for all this document represents. But the King of kings gives me the seal of His own body and blood to certify His word and His authority, to pledge all the power of God and heaven for that which is given me in His promise.

The lover gives his beloved a promise of love and loyalty and marriage. He then seals his promise with a visible pledge by his ring. My divine Lover also gives me His word of promise and forgiveness, but He seals that promise and His word with a visible pledge of His own body and blood, with which He loved me unto death.

The prodigal's father gives his repentant son his word of pardon, but he goes farther. He makes him a supper, he clothes him in a robe of honor, he places a golden ring upon his hand. So my Lord welcomes me to a glorious supper of reconciliation, in which He gives me His very self to eat and to drink, in which He clothes me in His own robe of righteousness, and in which He binds me to Himself with the bonds of everlasting love.

How can the sense of guilt dog me now? Dare my faith now waver? Shall I doubt His pardon? How can my conscience, that judge ever haling me before His tribunal for condemnation, trouble me any longer? For I have met my Lord in a most personal fellowship, in the most intimate communion with Him that I can ever experience on this side of heaven.

Luther once said about this "given for you": "Now bring yourself into this YOU." That is what my Lord Jesus helps me to do in His Supper. "Given for you" and "shed for your sins" are spoken to me, and I personally receive the very body that was given for me and the very blood that was shed for me. What more can Jesus do to assure me that I am the YOU whom He means? And what else can I do but to sink myself wholly and confidently into this YOU which He speaks to me in His Word as well as in the Sacrament of His body and His blood?

But some sincere Christian will tell me that he does not always leave the altar with complete assurance, with an untroubled conscience, with real peace of mind. What may be the cause?

Perhaps he mentally or unconsciously reserved a secret sin in his confession. Perhaps he did confess it but knew that he meant to love and to keep it at least a little longer when he promised to amend his sinful life. Perhaps he went home and remembered an enemy he had forgotten to forgive and was not ready to forgive, or a wrong that had been committed against him that he was not willing to forget.

Did he commune to his condemnation? God forbid! His confession was faulty, his faith was weak, his promise was lame. But it is the lame and the weak and the faulty whom the Lord wants to help. If the Communion did nothing more to him than to make him aware of his omissions it has awakened him to a true sense of sin and should drive him back to his Savior for forgiveness and to a subsequent better confession and soul-satisfying Communion, one that he can leave with true peace of mind.

I have also heard my Lord's command in the Holy Supper: "This do in remembrance of Me." I recall the story of two boys, fast friends, one a consecrated Christian and the other a likeable but careless worldling. All the persuasions of the Christian were of little avail with the worldling. Then one night the bad boy decided to drive to a very questionable resort and could not be dissuaded by his friend, whom he left in anger after a stormy argument. Upon his return he met with an accident that killed his companion and pinned him under his burning automobile. The Christian boy at home, praying and hoping for his friend's safe return, seemed called by some unseen power to go out and seek him. Thus he found him under the car from which he could not extricate himself. Unable to find anything to use as a lever to lift the car, the Christian crept under it, making a lever of his back and released his friend, only to be severely burned before he could release himself. The story ends with the saved boy exclaiming: "You saved my life at the risk of your own. Now I belong to you, and from this day I will listen to you and take your advice and try to follow your ideals."

As I take my departure from the Communion altar I hear my Savior's words: "Remember Me." And I remember how His love constrained Him to lay down His life for me, and how again He gives me His very body and blood with which He lifted me out of death into eternal life.

This remembering I must carry with me from this Communion to the next. This remembering must go into action. His ideals must be mine. I must listen to Him, I must obey Him. Must? Why, it should be the joy of my life to do so. And besides, do I not take with me from the Table of the Lord a heavenly food—the bread of life and the wine of salvation that strengthen me not only to remember my Savior but to live my Christ?

There was once a good bishop who to the end of his life, whenever he administered Communion, trembled in awe of the sacred mystery with which he as a steward of God had been entrusted. But when he had sent the last communicant away, a sudden great exaltation overcame him, and a peace that was beyond understanding filled his soul.

O Holy Spirit, give me such a sense of the sacredness and the life-giving power of the great sacramental mystery that my soul, too, may tremble in awe over my Lord's real presence, so that I might want to cry out with Peter, "Depart from me, for I am a sinful man, O Lord." And then send me away from the altar filled with a sense of the peace which passeth understanding and a sense of the power which strengthens me to fight the good fight of faith unto the end so that I might also cry out with Paul, "I can do all things through Christ which strengtheneth me."

Faithful Father in heaven! How good Thou hast been to me to permit me to become one of the "whosoevers" that believe in Thine only-begotten Son whom Thou hast sent into the world to save perishing men and to give them everlasting life! May Thine infinite love beget in my heart a love that overflows upward unto Thee and outward unto lost humanity.

Beloved Jesus! How good Thou art to me that Thou permittest me to become one of the "You's" for whom Thou gavest Thyself for the remission of sin, and that Thou still givest Thy precious body and blood to me to eat and to drink for the blessed assurance of forgiveness and salvation and life! O Lamb of God! May the remembrance of Thy sacrifice upon the cross and the gift of Thy Sacrament draw me in love and devotion to Thy side and keep my life secure.

Precious Holy Spirit! How good Thou art to me that Thou makest me a repenter, a confessor, and a believer, and that Thou leadest me into the Holy of Holies, there to be sprinkled with the blood of the Lamb of God that taketh away the sins of the world! And now, Thou mover of the gospel pen, keep what Thou hast written into my heart, the pardon of the spoken gospel and the power of the sacramental gospel, so that I may live a blessed and sanctified life to the glory of God the Father, Son, and Holy Ghost. Amen.

Introducing the Authors

Amos John Traver is Professor of Practical Theology at Hamma Divinity School, Springfield, Ohio. He also serves as chairman of the Division of Public Relations of the National Lutheran Council and is a member of the Board of Publication, U.L.C.A. He is the author of a number of books, including *Harvesters, Lutheran Handbook,* and *What A Church Member School Do,* and for the past ten years has contributed comments on the International Sunday School Lessons for the *Christan Herald.* He is a frequent contributor to *The Lutheran* and other periodicals.

Otto A. Geiseman hails from Sioux City, Iowa, and has had an outstanding ministry at Grace Lutheran Church, River Forest, Illinois, since 1922. Pastor Geiseman is well known as an author and lecturer. His most recent books were: *Make Yours A Happy Marriage, For Peace Within,* and *Old Truths For A New Day.* He is author of the column "This Day" and is a member of the Family Life Committee, Lutheran Church-Missouri Synod.

E. E. Ryden has served as Editor of *The Lutheran Companion,* official organ of the Augustana Lutheran Church, for the past 20 years. At present he is also serving as president of the Board of Directors of Augustana College, Rock Island, Illinois, and as secretary of the Joint Commission on the Common Hymnal. He is author of *The Story Of Our Hymns* and has recently written an important series of articles on "The Common Hymnal." He was educated at Augustana College and Seminary and in 1948 served as a representative of the Augustana Lutheran Church at the World Council of Churches in Amsterdam.

George W. Krueger is Lutheran service pastor in San Antonio, Texas, and chaplain of Grace Lutheran Sanatorium in the same city. He has served as chairman of the Board of American Missions and as ranking vice-president of the Illinois District, American Lutheran Church. He is author of *Out Of The Depths, Wartime Prayers For Christians,* and contributes to "Portals of Prayer." He is a graduate of Wartburg College, Waverly, Iowa, and Wartburg Seminary, Dubuque, Iowa.

C. U. Wolf is a native of Maryland and pastor of St. Paul Lutheran Church, Toledo, Ohio. He is presently serving as vice-president of the Toledo Archaeological Society and chairman of the Committee on Counselling of the Toledo Council of Churches. Until recently he was professor of Old Testament Theology at Maywood Seminary. He has written articles for *The Lutheran Church Quarterly*, *Jewish Quarterly Review,* and *The Pulpit,* and is author of the book *Freddie.*

John O. Lang is pastor of St. Paul's Lutheran Church, Columbus, Ohio, and lecturer in Liturgics at Capital University Seminary. He has also taught German and history at Capital University. He has written articles for *The Lutheran Outlook* and *The Pastor's Monthly* and was a contributor to the book *At Jesus' Feet.* He is a graduate of Capital University and Seminary, Columbus, Ohio.

Wm. L. Young is executive secretary of the Board of Higher Education, American Lutheran Church, and also secretary of the Joint Union Merger Committee. He is past president of the National Lutheran Education Conference and for one year served as acting president of Capital University. Dr. Young has written articles on religious and educational subjects and fills a busy schedule of lecture and speaking engagements. He is a graduate of Capital University and Ohio State University.

William D. Streng is a native of Dubuque, Iowa, and now serves as Professor of Christian Education at Wartburg Seminary in that city. He is dean of Luther Academy and advisor to the Board of Parish Education, American Lutheran Church. He is the author of various books and articles, including *Altars That Alter, Christian Education-Quest Or Gospel? Increasing Communion Attendance,* and *Christian Worship.* Professor Streng has served as lecturer on Evangelism for the National Lutheran Council and is the father of the Family Sunday School Plan.

W. A. Poovey is pastor of Ascension Lutheran Church, Memphis, Tenn., and serves as secretary of the Board for Christian Social Action, American Lutheran Church. He has written a number of religious plays and is author of *Questions That Trouble Christians* and *Problems That Plague The Saints.* He was educated at Capital University and Seminary and the Northwestern University School of Speech.

Ross H. Stover has been pastor of Messiah Lutheran Church, Philadelphia, Pa., for the past 35 years. At present he is also teacher of speech at Temple University. He is in wide demand as a speaker and annually fills speaking engagements throughout the United States.

He is author of *The Art Of Public Speaking, Three Cheers,* and *I'll Tell You Why I Am A Protestant,* among others. He has studied at Wittenberg, Hamma Divinity School, Temple University, and the American Seminary.

Petrus Olaf Bersell is president emeritus of the Augustana Lutheran Church. Among other offices he holds at present he serves as a member of the Central Board of the World Council of Churches and a member of the Executive Committee of the National Lutheran Council. He is a native of Rock Island, Illinois, and was educated in that city at Augustana College and Seminary. Dr. Bersell has filled three speaking engagements on the Columbia Church of the Air and spoke at youth conventions at Lutheran World Federation meetings in Lund and in Hannover.

Robert Henry Boyd is Professor of Old Testament at Luther Seminary, St. Paul, Minnesota. He has written articles for the *Lutheran Teacher, Friend of Zion,* and the *Lutheran Herald* and contributed a sermon for the book *In Whom We Live.* A native of Iowa, Dr. Boyd was educated at St. Olaf College, Luther Seminary, and Princeton University and Seminary.

O. P. Kretzmann has been president of Valparaiso University, Valparaiso, Ind., since 1940. His long list of other activities includes membership on the Midwest Conference of Atomic Scientists and Religious Leaders and secretaryship of the Board for Higher Education, Lutheran Church-Missouri Synod. Dr. Kretzmann is author of *The Road Back To God, Remember,* and *The Pilgrim;* editor of *The Cresset;* associate editor of *The American Lutheran.* A graduate of Concordia Seminary, St. Louis, Missouri, he has done postgraduate work at Harvard, Columbia, John Hopkins, and Chicago Universities.

Conrad Bergendoff is a native of Nebraska and has served as president of Augustana College since 1935. Educated at Augustana College and Seminary, the Universities of Pennsylvania and Chicago, Dr. Bergendoff has received an Honorary Doctor of Theology degree from Upsala University in Sweden. He is author of articles on theology, education, and history and is author of *The Making and Meaning Of The Augsburg Confession* and *Christ As Authority,* among others. Dr. Bergendoff has delivered the Dudlican Lectures at Harvard and the Hoover Lectures at the University of Chicago.

Gustav J. Neumann is vice-president of the college and head of the English Department at Wartburg College, Waverly, Iowa. He also serves as a member of the Board of Publication, American Lutheran Church; president of the Iowa Poetry Society, and poetry editor of the *Lutheran Standard*. He received his education at Wartburg College, the University of Berlin, and State University of Iowa. He is author of the books, *O Bethlehem, Thou Beautiful, O Little Babe of Bethlehem, The House of Wonder,* and *A Book Of Prayers For Boys And Girls.*

Lewis Holm is a native of Iowa and pastor of St. Paul's American Lutheran Church, Oklahoma City, Oklahoma. He has contributed articles and stories to the *Lutheran Standard* and was educated at Wartburg College and Wartburg Seminary.

Kurt Carl Hartmann is pastor of Immanuel Lutheran Church, Pflugerville, Texas, and serves as secretary of the Texas Lutheran College Board of Regents and as a member of the Texas Lutheran Welfare Society Board. He is author of articles in the *Lutheran Standard* and *The Lutheran Outlook* and the book *Calvary Conquering Christ.* He has also served as editor of *Worker's Exchange,* the official organ of Mexican Mission work in the American Lutheran Church. He is a graduate of Texas Lutheran College, Seguin, Texas, Wartburg Seminary, Dubuque, Iowa, and has studied at Texas A & M College and Edinburg College.

Edward W. Schramm has been editor of the *Lutheran Standard* for the past twenty-five years and is presently serving as vice-president of the National Lutheran Editors' Association. Dr. Schramm is a popular speaker and fills many engagements at Lutheran chautauquas, Bible camps, and district conventions. He is author of *What Shall I Do With Jesus? The Evening Sacrifice,* and editor of *At Jesus' Feet.* He received his education at Capital University and Seminary and Ohio State University.

George H. Muedeking hails from Wisconsin and for the past two years has served as pastor of Christ Lutheran Church, El Cerrito, California. He is also secretary of the California District of the American Lutheran Church and president of the National Lutheran Council Bay Area Pastors' Association. He is author of articles which have appeared in the *Lutheran Theological Quarterly, The Lutheran Outlook, Lutheran Standard,* and others. He has served as instructor in Christian Ethics at the University of California.

L. E. Eifert is an ordained pastor of the Lutheran Church-Missouri Synod and is presently serving as area representative for the Lutheran Service Commission. He has held pastorates in Anaheim and Laguna Beach, California. He is a graduate of Concordia College, St. Paul, Minnesota, and Concordia Seminary, St. Louis, Missouri.

G. E. Melchert has been pastor of Trinity American Lutheran Church, Waterloo, Iowa, since 1930. Dr. Melchert is famous as a radio preacher and has appeared on the program "Your Hour of Worship" every Sunday since 1936. He is a graduate of Wartburg College and Seminary and received his D.D. degree from Wartburg Seminary in 1949.

Herman Mees Meyer has been pastor of First Lutheran Church, Fullerton, California, for the past year. He has twice served as lecturer for Lutheran One-Day Seminars and in 1951 was chairman of the Committee on Lutheran One-Day Seminars for the American Lutheran Conference. He has contributed material for devotional books. He has studied at Capital University and Seminary, Columbia, Union Seminary, and the University of Edinburgh.

John E. Meyer has been associate pastor of St. John's Lutheran Church, San Antonio, Texas, for the past two years. He has written articles and stories which have appeared in *The Lutheran Outlook, One,* and *Christian Life.* Pastor Meyer's first pastorate was in a mission congregation in South Miami, Florida. He was educated at Wartburg College, Wartburg Seminary, and Capital Seminary.

George W. Scheid is a Lutheran layman, residing in Monroeville, Ohio, where he is assistant cashier of the Farmers and Citizens Banking Company. He was educated at the Commercial School of Ohio Northern University, Ada, Ohio, and has taught in elementary schools.